LIVING NATIONAL TREASURES

LIVING NATIONAL TREASURES

A celebration of British craftsmanship

through the eyes of COUNTRY LIFE

In association with

Howard de Walden Estates Limited

PAVILION

First published in Great Britain in 1997 by
PAVILION BOOKS LIMITED
26 Upper Ground, London SE1 9PD

Designed by the Bridgewater Book Company

A CIP catalogue record for this book is available from the British Library.

ISBN 1 86205 032 5

Typeset in Simoncini Garamond
Printed and bound by Conti Tipocolor in Italy

2 4 6 8 10 9 7 5 3 1

This book may be ordered by post direct from the publisher.
Please contact the Marketing Department.
But try your bookshop first.

Country Life magazine is published every Thursday by IPC Magazines Limited, Kings Reach Tower,
Stamford Street, London SE1 9LS. Subscription enquiries: Quadrant Subscription Services,
Oakfield House, 35 Perrymount Road, Haywards Heath, West Sussex RH16 3DH.
Tel: 01444 445555

Contents

FOREWORD   6

INTRODUCTION   7

PORTRAITS   12

GALLERY   112

ADDRESSES   132

INDEX   142

ACKNOWLEDGEMENTS   144

Foreword

Shortly before I became editor of *Country Life*, the late Gervase Jackson-Stops told me about the Japanese system of recognizing Living National Treasures. These, he said, were figures whom the government wished to honour as masters of great craft skills. We agreed that there were many people in Britain with wonderful skills that similarly deserved celebrating. This was the spirit in which *Country Life's* series of Living National Treasures, edited by Melanie Cable-Alexander, started four years ago. Since then we have come to realize that the cornucopia of specialist ability that exists in Britain is well nigh inexhaustible. Certainly there is no sign that we are likely to run out of Treasures (as we affectionately call them) and we are proud to continue the series week by week.

This book is a record of the Treasures whom we have published to date. A glance at it will show the variety of skills that still flourish in this country, from bagpipe-making to thatching. We have generally favoured craftsmen who create new things. Britain is also remarkable for its expertise in the different fields of conservation, in many of which it leads the world. What we have wanted to publish, though, are those skills that still form a living tradition. We draw attention to that word 'living': sadly, a number of our Treasures have no one to whom they can pass on their knowledge. They believe that their crafts will perish when they retire. We hope that this book will not just commemorate our Treasures, but spread the message that their skills must not be lost.

Perhaps the list of addresses and telephone numbers (see pages 132–141) will assist this process, by allowing readers to commission work from the Treasures. We know from the number of readers who phone *Country Life* that there is a lively interest from the public in acquiring the services of Treasures, once they know that they exist. We also hope that some means can be found of matching unemployed young people, who would often dearly love to work with their hands, with Treasures who might be willing to train them in their craft. Britain should glory in its craftsmanship. The economic future for it looks promising. An attraction of the Treasure's métier is that it can never be superseded by machine.

We see this book as a directory of the Treasures so far published by *Country Life*. Sadly, since we first launched the series, some Treasures have retired and others have died, and these people are not included in the book. We have chosen 50 photographs to show at a larger size, simply because we felt them to be particularly successful as photographs. Size of photograph does not imply a value judgement about the Treasures depicted. We had always thought that our Living National Treasures series might one day make a book, but it was the enthusiasm of Andrew Ashenden that persuaded us to do something about it. I am immensely grateful to him for having made publication financially possible, and to Melanie Cable-Alexander, without whose genius for spotting appropriate Treasures this book, which she has compiled, would not have been possible.

CLIVE ASLET

Editor, *Country Life*

Introduction

'Good work proceeding from the whole man;
heart, head and hand in proper balance.'

Soetsu Yanagi, 1972

Britain is, and always has been, extraordinarily good at tradition and craftsmanship. Since 1993 *Country Life* has included a feature each week illustrating a wide range of skills, under the title 'Living National Treasure'. This series has proved to be extremely popular and clearly lends itself to the creation of a book. Howard de Walden Estates has decided to sponsor its publication.

The original idea for the Living National Treasures series came from Japan, where each spring the government publishes a form of honours list of men and women working in traditional arts and crafts who are seen to be preserving an important section of the country's cultural heritage. These men and women are awarded the title *Ningen Kokuho* or 'Living National Treasure'. Borrowing this idea, *Country Life* launched its own series in February 1993, identifying each week individuals deserving an accolade for preserving a skill of great excellence and rarity – in some cases, the person selected is the last operating within his or her field. If this book can in some way help to preserve these occupations, and hopefully make a contribution to a more secure future for them, then it will have been immensely worthwhile.

In a leading article in *Country Life*, editor Clive Aslet highlighted the remarkable depth and breadth of the nation's skill in a huge range of activities; amazingly, these achievements are often not properly recognized or appreciated, and yet they survive against all the odds. Sadly, we may be living on borrowed time, as many practitioners were trained decades ago and young people are not taking up their trades.

The reasons for this are numerous and complex, the most obvious being the lack of attractive apprenticeship schemes to encourage new blood to learn such skills, which take many years to achieve. In addition there is the lack of status and recognition, often coupled with poor financial reward. The response to *Country Life*'s Living National Treasures series shows that there is no shortage of demand for such skills, when they are drawn to public notice, but frequently the buying public remains unaware of the range of remarkable skills available to it. It is hoped that this book will improve such awareness and generate increased interest in a sector of the British economy that should be valued and appreciated far more than it is.

The sponsorship of this book by Howard de Walden Estates has come about because of the company's interest in preserving and encouraging the unique traditions of Britain and also because, as a business, it is very involved in the repair and refurbishment of listed and historic buildings. For example, in the repair and restoration of buildings, the skill of the brick maker who constructs by hand is often called upon when matching bricks are required, and the nail maker may be asked to solve a roofing problem. Many buildings owned by Howard de Walden Estates have important internal details, and the skills of the plasterer, gilder and carver, as well as those of other building specialists, are frequently required.

The company's archivists commission bookbinders and restorers to ensure that important documents are properly stored and preserved. It is refreshing and fascinating to work with people who are so committed to their occupation – in some cases obsessively so – and whose sole objective is to produce a result that is correct in all aspects. The nature of Howard de Walden Estates is such that it takes the long-term view of its activities, and therefore seeks the skills that not only solve problems in the traditional way, but also ensure that the quality and accuracy of the work mean that it will last as long as was intended and will be pleasing both to the touch and to the eye.

Everyone included in this book deserves praise, because he or she is preserving a skill of excellence that should be nurtured and encouraged as a precious part of our way of life. Inevitably, it is possible to include only a limited number of practitioners, but *Living National Treasures* still provides an indication of the astonishing range of skills and abilities available today and so often overlooked in this era of high technology. It would be all too easy to assume that there are very few traditional craftsmen currently at work, but, as this book demonstrates, there are still a remarkable number quietly pursuing their chosen occupation with great dedication.

Each has the desire to maintain unmatched quality and high standards, and to do the job to the best of his or her ability. These craftsmen have in the main ignored the distorted priorities of the past quarter-century and have concentrated instead on fulfilling their particular role in life, usually with modest material reward, but with immense satisfaction to themselves and their clients. They are hard-working and independent, the latter quality no doubt arising from the isolation and the increasing rarity of many of their particular occupations.

Our national Treasures defy imitation. All the remarkable people included here have a strong personal influence on what they do and make. Modern quality and durability may be impressive, but lack the subtle individuality and uniqueness created by the traditional practitioner. Modern machinery and technology benefit the economy and therefore general standards of living, but our quality of life suffers from the relentless loss of traditional techniques and of the high standards of individual skills.

Today the world is obsessed with speed and accountability, which often results in poor quality and corner-cutting, and in the long run frequently means an unsatisfactory project. The individuals portrayed in this book illustrate a somewhat overlooked, but vitally important, sector of our economy, which keeps alive Britain's traditions and its uniqueness in the world – and these are far too precious to be allowed to wither. Every time a traditional occupation is allowed to die for lack of a successor, something of immense value is lost from our heritage, and the community is left that much poorer.

Many books have been published on crafts and craftsmen, but this one concentrates on a wider sector, incorporating numerous people who uphold a particular task or occupation that is steeped in history and tradition. It is aimed not only at creating a visually attractive and interesting read, but also at drawing the attention of a wider audience to the activities of these special people. It is not intended to be a reference book, but relevant addresses are included, together with a telephone hotline enabling readers to make further enquiries and obtain additional information.

Living National Treasures is not just about the craft of making things; it is also about traditional occupations that are an essential and intricate part of community life. So many of our best-loved activities depend on dedicated and knowledgeable individuals, and without them our enjoyment of life would be hugely diminished. These people deserve our recognition and respect, and above all our encouragement, to ensure that their skills survive. They are not practising something which is old-fashioned, quaint or obsolete – they are using very ancient skills and talents which are increasingly in demand today. We must not overlook them in our headlong charge towards a society of high technology and information overload.

ANDREW ASHENDEN

Managing Director

Howard de Walden Estates

IN THE EARLY 1940s *Country Life* published an article bemoaning the decline of the ancient craft of thatching. It featured master craftsman David Turbitt as one of the few remaining skilled thatchers. Today his sons, David junior and Frank, follow in his footsteps, continuing a tradition established by his family in George II's reign.

Thatcher

Frank Turbitt says that thatching was not his chosen career. 'I wanted to farm. But when my brother went off to do his National Service, my father kept on at me to help out with the thatching. That was how I became involved, and I wouldn't think of doing anything else now.'

He and his brother worked for their father until the 1970s, when they set up on their own, united in their determination to keep thatching skills alive in Devon, where their family has always lived. They are positive about their role and about the future of the Turbitt family tradition – with good reason. David has a son who is already a thatcher, and Frank has a son waiting in the wings.

PRIMITIVE ARCHITECTURE provided inspiration for the rustic huts that were built in eighteenth- and nineteenth-century English landscaped parks as the setting for diversions and picnics. David and Andrew Raffle are among the last people in the country to make summerhouses in this tradition. They repaired the Moss House (see photograph, right), which was commissioned in about 1820 for the Spring Garden at Belvoir Castle, Lincolnshire.

Rustic-Hut Maker

Both brothers served apprenticeships as thatchers in Derbyshire, but in 1983 they decided to specialize in building and restoring rustic huts. After much historical research, they embarked on designing their own. 'We thatch with heather, straw or reed, and we use timber which still has the bark on it,' says David Raffle (*left*). 'Some people ask us to put in a hidden door, so we build in a bit of curved wood which can act as a door handle, opening into a secret storage space behind.' The brothers intend their summerhouses to seem as natural as possible: 'We like creating the excitement of nature tamed – but only just.'

FOR YEARS BOX (*Buxus*) was a neglected shrub in Britain. The occasional rare variety was found in botanic gardens, but few varieties were available commercially. That was until Elizabeth Braimbridge decided to address the problem in 1973. She has single-handedly rekindled an interest in the plant and established herself as

Rare-Plant Conservator

the leading authority in the country on box. At her nursery near Liss, in Hampshire, she has a unique library of different varieties and species. Many of her specimens come from abroad, from as far-flung reaches as South Africa, Japan, America and Cuba.

Mrs Braimbridge also clips complex designs in box. She has initialled QPR for a Queen's Park Rangers football fan and sculpted a life-size racing car for the well-known drummer of a pop group. 'Box is a fascinating plant,' she says. 'It is very plain and low-key, which is why it is such a classic. It reflects the light well and comes into its own during winter. It is the heart of the garden and you can also treat it as a lovely amusing thing.'

TELEVISION WEATHERMEN may not have forecast the hurricane of 1987, but octogenarian Bill Foggitt knew something was afoot. The night before, his cat started jumping about: 'Blackie always does that before strong *Weatherman* winds come.'

Mr Foggitt is a naturalist. By studying the birds and the bees he learns the facts of life about the weather. 'I keep a pine cone outside my door. Open scales show that dry weather is on the way. When they close, it will be damp and windy.' This may sound like an old wives' tale, but his work is taken seriously. He supplies daily information to the Meteorological Office and has been a television weather presenter.

Mr Foggit's fascination with the weather is in his genes. Thomas Jackson Foggitt (1812–85) was the first Foggitt to keep weather records – his diaries are in Mr Foggitt's safekeeping, as are his grandfather's, father's and uncle's. But Mr Foggitt's interest in the climate was sparked in 1927 by the last total eclipse, which he witnessed with his father and grandfather from a boat at sea. 'You'd better take notes,' his father said, 'because I won't be around for the next one.'

JACK HOUSE has been ploughing with horses since the age of fourteen, when he started work on a farm at Downton, Wiltshire. 'We used to spend most of the winter ploughing,' he says. Like his father and grandfather before him, he used Shires to pull grass-cutters, corn-cutters, binders and hay wagons.

Since 1950 Mr House has had his own smallholding at Quidhampton, near Salisbury. He breeds a Shire foal nearly every year. 'In the old days, working with two horses abreast and a single-furrow plough, we aimed to plough an acre a day,' he says.

Ploughman

Today he concentrates principally on competing, participating in more than a dozen competitions per year – he is a past winner of the All England Ploughing Championship. But he still believes that 'Horse ploughing is far superior to tractor ploughing. It is much nicer to work with horses, and traditional ploughing methods are much less damaging to the soil.'

IT MUST BE CONFUSING to have two people called Thomas working with you, but eighty-one-year-old George Hall has no objections to it, for the pair are members of his family – his son and grandson. All are renowned for their stonewalling work throughout Northumberland.

Stonewalling is like doing a jigsaw puzzle, according to Hall senior. 'You need to know

Drystone Waller

your stones and you have to pick the right pieces from the pile. Each stone has to cover the join of the two beneath it.' The type of stone used – limestone, whin, sandstone – depends on the location of the wall and is chosen to blend in with the landscape. A good day for one man would mean completing 4–5 yards, and the average height of a wall is 4½–5 feet.

The team uses a frame to get the shape right, ensuring that the wall tapers from 24 inches wide at the bottom to 14 inches at the top. Cement is used on the top of the wall to prevent cattle knocking off the stones, but the wall's overall stability depends on the skill of the craftsmen. 'It's like a monument. We build something that should last for a hundred years.'

JONATHAN AND RAY WRIGHT are a father-and-son team who work the ancient mine at Clearwell Cave in the Forest of Dean. It is the only working iron mine in the forest and the Wrights are granted the privilege of working it because they are freeminers. To become a freeminer is a complicated process, as Wright senior explains:

Freeminer

'You have to be a male over the age of twenty-one who has worked for a year and a day in a mine in a forest; you also have to be born within the hundred of St Briavells.' The 'hundred' is a reference to the medieval method of dividing the country into areas where the king could locate a hundred fighting men.

Mr Wright was born just outside the hundred, but he is officially known as secretary of the Freeminers' Association, having become a freeminer by purchase some three decades ago – he bought the right to a freeminer's tenure from the Crown. He is also a verderer of the forest.

'I much prefer working in iron mines,' he says. 'People who take out coal are not really miners, they are colliers. We still mine tons of coloured ochres, which artists use for painting and restoring old murals, and we open the cave up to the public.'

'IWOULD RECOGNIZE a house from our bricks anywhere,' says Bill Watkinson, who started work at Michelmersh Brick Company, the Hampshire company famous for its hand-made bricks, in 1938. David Hill, who owns the company, estimates that Mr Watkinson has hand-made enough bricks during his career to build at least 1,500 houses.

The skill of the 'hand-maker', as they are called in the trade, is to ensure that the mixture of clay, sand and coal

Brick Maker

dust completely fills the brick moulds. At his peak, Mr Watkinson averaged about 7,000 bricks a week. He no longer makes bricks himself, but carries out special orders. 'Someone once asked for two Ferrari cars to be carved into the brick to go either side of their front gate,' he says.

The most expensive single brick he made cost £320, and was used in restoring an old country house. Listed buildings in particular need bricks of a precise colour, size and shape. Cathedrals, castles and the Prime Minister's official country residence, Chequers, have all benefited from his labour. According to Mr Watkinson, hand-made bricks are superior to machine-made as they provide better insulation, are more durable and more attractive to look at. 'If you look at the viaducts built in the last century you will see that they are still in perfect condition.'

R UPERT REA is leading, almost single-handedly, a revival in the ancient craft of nail making. His principal role is as an engineer but, whenever he finds an odd moment, he practises a skill that died out more than a century ago. 'It all came about because of the Avoncroft Museum of Historic Buildings, Worcestershire, which bought up an old nail shop from Bromsgrove, where the museum is based,' Mr Rea explains.

'Back in 1850 there were 3,500 nail makers in

Nail Maker

Bromsgrove; it was really a local industry. I became interested in this shop because my grandparents used to be nail makers and it seemed a shame to leave the machinery gathering dust. I started researching how nails were made, which took about two years. Now I put on demonstrations at the museum.'

A hand-made nail starts life as a 20-inch length of mild steel, which is forged into a point and moulded using a treadle hammer. Each takes an average of thirty seconds to construct. 'There is quite a demand for hand-made nails for restorers of old buildings and furniture. The possibilities are limitless.'

IF CLARK KENT IS SUPERMAN, then Keith Garnett is Super-rigger, for he created all the wires for the hero's moves. Lives literally depend upon him. 'I do all the rigging and wire-work for Gerry Cottle's circus, too. When I see performers hanging thirty to forty feet up, suspended on my ropes, it does give me a bit of a shock.'

Mr Garnett, however, should be used to seeing people hanging from ropes. *Rigger* His first job was with the Merchant Navy, where, at the age of fifteen, he learnt to make the lines used in sailing ships. 'It was excellent training. But this work takes years to learn. You also need a good head for maths, because you have to work out all the right tonnages and angles.' He once had to create a rope strong enough to suspend an 8-ton box containing some dozen actors for a National Theatre production. He also works regularly for the Royal Opera House. But his favourite commission was to redo the wires used to raise the front of Queen Mary's doll's house at Windsor Castle. 'They had deteriorated badly and I spent a morning at Windsor fixing them. I have a letter somewhere from the Palace thanking me for it.'

Mr Garnett's assistant in the photograph is Rani, a famous circus elephant. Rani is now enjoying a happy retirement in Spain.

THERE ARE HINTS of the twentieth century in the moulding shop of the Whitechapel Bell Foundry where Danny Matholus works. The blare of Radio 1 mingles with the sound of chiming bells from the tuning department. But the technique used to make the bells has remained essentially unchanged since the foundry was established in the fifteenth century.

'First we form the core, the mould to make the inside shape of the bell, from loam and curved bricks,' Mr Matholus explains. 'Then the cope, also made of loam, is formed inside a cast-iron moulding case.' Each mould, smoothed to the precise shape required by means of curved moulding boards

Bell Founder

called strickles, is then filled with glowing molten bronze, trundled out from the foundry furnace in a massive ladle. Enormous, fin-shaped strickles, which hang on the foundry wall like trophies from a shark-fishing expedition, commemorate the biggest bell ever cast: 13½-ton Big Ben.

The mechanics of bell founding fill Mr Matholus with pride, and since he joined the foundry on a salary of 30 pence an hour in 1966 he has made some 2,000 bells. But does he like the sound of them? 'Not especially,' he admits, breaking into a twinkling smile.

JOHN RUDD'S GRANDFATHER began making hay rakes at his home town in Cumbria more than a hundred years ago. Now Mr Rudd and his son produce some 12,000–14,000 rakes a year, thanks largely to the machines that his father installed shortly after the Second World War.

Ash is used for the head and the supporting hoop, which is shaped after being softened in boiling water. Ramin wood is imported from the Far East for the shaft, and hard-wearing silver birch is used for the sixteen teeth. The wood is untreated and the rakes are assembled with only four nails. A rake in this sturdy design will last for many years – 'unless it meets with an accident,' says Mr Rudd.

Hay-Rake Maker

The rakes are bought by farmers and gardeners, but they are also used in athletics stadiums, on golf courses, by council workers and in window displays; angry peasants have waved them in historical dramas, and they have even been used by the police in a murder inquiry.

Farrier

BERNARD TIDMARSH'S FAMILY has been operating a business at the forge at Crudwell, Wiltshire, for 400 years. Many of the original tools still exist, including a lathe used to turn hubs when a wheelwright worked there with a blacksmith. It is a heritage of which Mr Tidmarsh is proud, but sadly one that will not necessarily last. 'I have a young daughter, but I doubt she will want to take over,' he says.

Mr Tidmarsh ventured into the business aged two and became a fully fledged apprentice at fifteen. 'I have never thought of doing anything else.' The forge has always been busy. In the old days, it was on the main route from the north to the south coast and attracted passing trade. 'The road outside the forge is now too busy to unbox horses on, so I use Badminton or my cottage, where I have a shoeing floor.'

His clientele includes the Duke of Badminton, competitors to the Badminton three-day event, which Mr Tidmarsh has attended since 1952, Olympic riders and three neighbouring Royal householders. In fact, it was through HRH The Prince of Wales that Mr Tidmarsh met his wife: she was the Prince's groom.

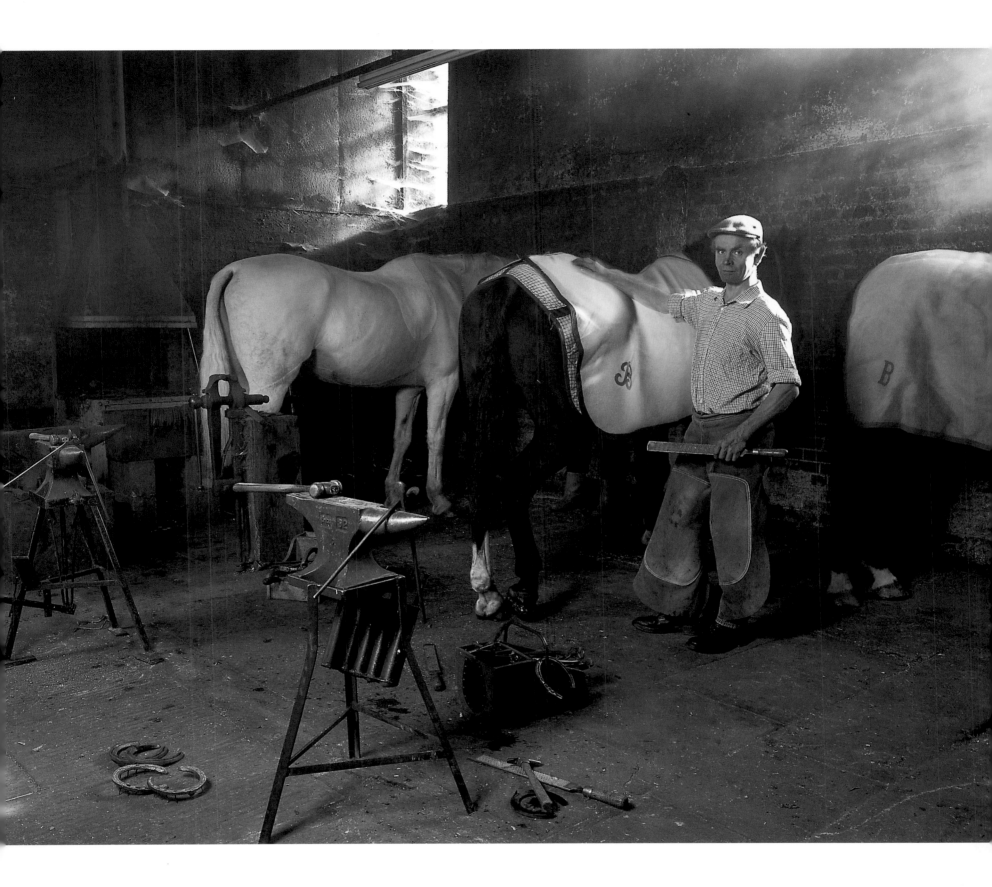

PEOPLE SAY THAT BRUCE DURNO communicates with hounds by telepathy, such is his skill as huntsman of the Fernie Hunt; followers credit him with supernatural powers. 'He is simply the best in the country,' the Earl of Onslow says.

Huntsman

'You will never meet another like him.'

A man of few words, Mr Durno is modest about his talents. 'All you need is the skill to handle a pack of hounds, and to be a good horseman so you can get across country. I was lucky because I was born and bred into hunting. My grandfather was a gamekeeper and my father was in hunt service with the Heythrop.'

Mr Durno has been riding to hounds since 1966 and originally started working as second whipper-in to the Heythrop. He usually hunts with a mixed pack. 'All the hounds have their own characters. Some are always quite close to you and looking at you, others will be off into the covert. I can recognize a few of their voices, but it might take me a little while.' Two of his favourite bitches are the sisters Softly and Socket. 'When anybody comes in, they will be the first to jump up and they are especially keen to say hello to children.'

A NY SADDLER BASED IN LEICESTERSHIRE has the advantage of being surrounded by some of the best hunting country in England. S. Milner & Son, near Melton Mowbray, has more than that to recommend it. It is one of the few remaining, and oldest, manufacturers of traditional bespoke saddles in the country.

Saddler

Generations of hunting families have flocked to Milners since it was first established in 1870. But the secret of its success lies not so much in loyal clientele, but in the family's ability to produce a strong male line. The present owners, Frank and Roger Milner, are the great-grandsons of the original founder. And there is another Milner in the wings: Frank's son Andrew. 'When my grandfather moved the business to Leicester in 1928, there were four other saddlers in the area, but they have since dropped out because they did not have the younger men coming in to take over,' Frank says.

It takes twelve weeks or more to have a Milner saddle made and fitted, and for both horse and rider it is a similar sensation to being kitted out with a bespoke Savile Row suit. 'The method we use is exactly the same as the company used a century ago, but with modern materials. We start by measuring the horse. Then we make the seat and have another fitting with horse and rider to take patterns for the flap. We take patterns for the panel and the final result is a saddle unique to you.' But there is a price for comfort – around £1,000.

R AY CORNE HAS BEEN MAKING HATS since he was twelve. He studied the trade under his father, who ran a family business that was brought to this country from France by Mr Corne's grandfather. Within the business, a certain Mr Patey was also learning the trade. In the late 1950s he set up his own shop in London, taking the young Mr Corne with him. The company that the pair established is now known throughout the world as a traditional hat maker and is noted for its hunting and riding caps.

As anyone who has sat for a fitting at Patey's will know, it is a formidable process. The hat maker moulds a spiked, metal

Riding-Hat Maker

contraption, a century-old conformateur, on to the head with all the finesse of a Victorian brain surgeon – at least, it feels like that at the time. The pattern taken will last a lifetime and the hat made from it will be secure enough to defy a gale.

Mr Corne says that it takes years to learn to make hats properly. 'An apprenticeship for a top hat alone is seven years.' The technique is to create a mould and put layers of linen over it. The finishes vary, depending on the type of hat: theatrical, Chelsea Pensioner, top hat or riding cap. Mr Corne's favourites are those he makes for period dramas. 'I went to art school when I was younger,' he explains. 'It requires an artistic streak to make these kinds of hats from old sketches.'

D ANIEL TIMMINS (*LEFT*) AND KEITH LEVETT are coat makers for Henry Poole and Company, the oldest and largest family-run firm of bespoke tailors in London, which supplies livery for the Royal Household and Mews. It takes four to six weeks for them to make a full state-coachman's outfit, but at least five years to learn how to craft it.

'It requires a great deal of patience to make these coats,' explains Mr Levett. 'But I love the idea that you are able to

Coat Maker

take seemingly random pieces of cloth and turn them into something as spectacular as a coachman's outfit, and they will be around a lot longer than my lifetime.' The pattern is taken from 'a beaten-up old coat from the Palace'. The cloth includes scarlet doeskin, velveteen and 2 per cent gold lace. The cut varies slightly from coat to coat, but they are essentially the same as they would have been at the turn of the last century, when the current models were first designed.

KATHLEEN CLIFFORD IS HEAD WIG MAKER at Ede & Ravenscroft, purveyors of ceremonial robes since 1689, and of wigs since 1726, when Thomas Ravenscroft established the business in London. 'The company makes more than 1,500 wigs a year, in five different designs, for people in the legal profession around the world,' she explains. 'Two designs – our barrister's wigs and full-bottomed wigs – were patented by Thomas Ravenscroft's grandson, Humphrey, in 1822 and 1835. The other designs are for coroners, judges and judge advocates.'

The wigs are made from horsehair and silk. As most are made to order, the firm has a complete record of every head for which

Wig Maker

they have been constructed. 'We need to record the head size in order to know which of our hundred or so wooden forms, many of which date from the last century, should be used.' Mrs Clifford was introduced to wig making by one of her school teachers, who used to weave hair at home for the wigs for Ede & Ravenscroft. 'I was not taught all the techniques until I became head wig maker – some of Humphrey Ravenscroft's techniques are still kept secret. Only three of us know the precise time for which the hair needs to be boiled if the curls are to keep their shape.'

Mrs Clifford is proud of the company's high standards: 'I know that if they look after their wigs properly, the newly qualified of today will never come back to us for another – unless, of course, they make the bench.'

ALBERT HODGES WAS DELIGHTED to be offered the position of butler to General Lord Ismay in 1933, when he was just twenty years old. However, he had one reservation. 'With so many women in the household, I was concerned that I would be kept under petticoat government.' Lord Ismay assured him that he himself had been *Butler* under the same regime for years. 'He said, "Albert, you look after me and I promise to look after you." That formed a bond of trust, which lasted throughout our life together.'

Lord Ismay became chief of staff and military adviser to Winston Churchill, then first Secretary-General to NATO. He died in 1965, but Mr Hodges recalls their partnership with affection. 'Not many men have had the opportunity of serving such a perfect employer, as well as enjoying good health, good fortune and the friendship of a great man.'

He does, however, recall one incident with embarrassment. 'I had driven Lord and Lady Ismay to Windsor Castle for luncheon with HM The Queen. Everything was serene and the band of the Coldstream Guards was playing. As I got out of my seat to open the door, I accidentally pressed the horn. Lady Ismay commented: "You seem to be making sure that our arrival does not go unnoticed."'

KEVIN MULVANY AND SUSAN ROGERS first met at their university Freshers' Ball. Unlike most students, who spend the rest of their university days ruing their initial attempts at friendships, they married, and formed a partnership making exquisite reproductions of historic houses and palaces. They are reproducing five European palaces for an American museum. Each takes a year to complete.

Model Maker

The pair use wood, resin, plaster 'and lots of Polyfilla' as their main materials and, remarkably, are self-taught. 'Shortly after leaving university, we found an old doll's house in a flea-market. We did it up, then began making doll's houses for shops. Because we had both trained as architectural historians, we wanted to put in more architectural detail, and so we moved on to private commissions,' Susan explains.

'We have to be flexible in the way we think, because we do not use orthodox methods. We carve, cast, practise carpentry and joinery, but we have never been trained in any of these skills.' All the models are made to a scale of 1:12 but, because the palaces they copy are so large, the models are never exact replicas. 'We take the main section and some of the principal state rooms to capture the essence of the building. Our models are interpretations, as opposed to reproductions.'

ERIC THROSSELL is an architect, historian, classicist and conservator. He also practises a rare and dying art form: rendered architectural drawing. 'It is a wonderful form of presentation, and a superb way of recording architecture for posterity,' he says. Rendered architectural drawing originated during the eighteenth century. Robert Adam would have employed several draughtsmen to do drawings for him. 'It was a way of showing a client what his building would eventually look like.'

Architectural Draughtsman

Mr Throssel works in ink or pencil on paper rendered sepia, or in watercolour, and several of his drawings have been hung at the Royal Academy's Summer Exhibition. The origins of his interest in the medium are more humble. At the age of fourteen he went to the Brixton School of Building, London. 'I had a wonderful art master who inspired my interest in the subject – I still have my first drawing, which I did in 1935. It is my favourite way of passing the time.'

Few architects practise the craft because computers have taken over. But Mr Throssell's work is safe for posterity: 'I will eventually hand all my work to the county record office, so future historians and architects can refer to it.'

T HE ROUTE TO THE HEART of a great house is through a mix of study and intuition, Jonathan Myles-Lea believes. To do justice to a building's peculiar character, an artist should approach it from both these perspectives. He laughingly remembers a time in 1992 when he was so wrapped up in painting Plas Teg, the huge Jacobean house in North Wales where he was then living, that he lost touch with national news and, misunderstanding a chance remark, was convinced for two months that the Liberal Democrat Party was in government.

Country-House Painter

'I was working for the owner and talented restorer Cornelia Bayley, who was a real inspiration to me,' he said. They often worked relentlessly into the night, restoring a magnificent Wyatt house in Shropshire and opening Plas Teg to the public at weekends. Mr Myles-Lea painted in the basement, and six macaws had the freedom of the servants' hall.

In 1996 his pictures were included in 'The Artist and the Country House' exhibition at Sotheby's. He now lives in a converted chapel in Wales, and has been busy painting Burghley House, Lincolnshire. 'I stayed there a couple of times and was left alone to explore it. Gradually, as you get to know a house, it is almost as if it speaks to you.'

P RACTICAL KNOW-HOW is as necessary as artistic ability in Christine Palmer's job. 'There is the right way and the wrong way to sharpen a chisel,' she says. Christine, a Quaker, works for Carvers and Gilders, a London-based company that she formed in 1979 with friends from art college and which has since become one of the premier workshops in Britain. They make virtually anything, from Baroque, Regency or Georgian-style mirrors to pelmets,

Gilder and Carver

overmantels, brackets and coronas in classical style, and create their own designs.

Although she spent three years at art college in the early 1970s, Christine learnt the manual side of her trade at the City and Guilds of London Art School. 'When you do the practical work, you get your eye in on ornament. You begin to notice it in your environment, on buildings and fine furniture. Modern art is so minimalist it tends to look down on ornamentation.'

One of her most challenging projects was to make a copy of a chaise-longue in the Victoria and Albert Museum. 'It had to be an exact replica and took about four months to complete.' Some of the picture frames that the company has to restore are as big as four yards by three; others are miniatures. They all require the same skills, using gesso, clay, gold leaf and gilt. Experience gained while doing work for the Royal Family at Hampton Court has helped Mrs Palmer in a recently completed restoration project at Harewood House.

T ED KNELL once had to make a bronze sculpture of an athlete balance on its big toe – not an easy task, given that the sculpture weighed about quarter of a ton. But Mr Knell is known in the bronze foundry world as the man who makes the impossible possible, having had years of experience working with artists such as Jacob Epstein, Barbara Hepworth and Elisabeth Frink. 'Sometimes I have to advise artists to put a bit of grass or something at the bottom, so that a piece can balance properly,' he says.

Bronze Founder

Mr Knell began working in the business by accident when he visited a labour exchange after completing his National Service in the Sinai desert. 'The officer interviewing me said I would be highly suited to the job because of all the sand used in the production of sculpture.' Curiously, for a man who expresses a deep passion for his work, he says that he does not particularly like sculptures themselves – 'I always see each piece as a job.' But he is not completely immune to their charms, for he has an urge to create a sculpture garden at his foundry, Burleighfield Arts, in Buckinghamshire, which he helped establish in 1977 with two other partners.

There is a firm distinction in his mind between his role as a craftsman and that of the artist: he translates an artist's vision from plaster into bronze using the lost wax method or a sand cast – and there his artistry stops.

STEPHEN WELSH, like his father before him, practises the ancient art of pargeting, a decorative form of hand-modelled plasterwork found on many of the cottages and houses in his home county of Suffolk. Mr Welsh had his hands in plaster from an early age: 'As a six-year-old, I remember helping Dad with his repairs by mixing buckets of "lime putty" or "gypsum plasters".'

Pargeter

He left school at fifteen to help full-time in his father's business and recalls with some pride the occasion that convinced him of his life's vocation. 'I crafted a triple horseshoe-stamped pattern on a well-known racing trainer's property in Newmarket.'

Plasters can vary from the up-to-date to the more traditional. 'I often work with cow-hair mortars or gypsum, lime and hair.' Using his fingers, small brushes and trowels the size of palette knives, he designs and moulds the delicate friezes, which can last a hundred years. Friezes vary from parish to parish, and many are based on those that were originally conceived on the large estates. A particular favourite, which is peculiar to Mr Welsh's Suffolk coastal region, is 'the honeysuckle'.

L EONARD GRANDISON sometimes find himself restoring work originally completed by his grandfather, who established the family business, L. Grandison & Son, in Peebles in 1886 and specialized in doing ornamental plaster work. 'After 1914 there was little call for that,' says Mr Grandison, whose own son is also involved in the business. 'Most of our work now involves restoration and it is a big occasion when we get a chance to do something new.'

Plasterer

An impression is taken of the plasterwork using a latex material, which, because of its elasticity, does not damage the original. The plaster for exterior work is lime-based, because it is porous and less harmful to old buildings; otherwise they use plaster of Paris, and the most skilful part of the job is handling the wet plaster. 'I liken the craft to that of a potter or a glassblower, because it involves dexterity.' Whenever the Grandisons make a mould, they always keep the master. 'We have the biggest collection of its kind in Scotland.'

SOME OF THE BOOKS that Bill Topping restores and conserves are more than 1,000 years old. They belong to the rare books section of the Lambeth Palace library, where he has worked since 1964. 'Being a religious library, it is a quiet place with a relaxed atmosphere,' he says, 'perfect for a bookbinder.' As well as repairing and replacing spines and covers, Mr Topping is responsible for conserving damaged manuscripts.

Bookbinder

Pages are resewn using a traditional sewing frame and unbleached thread on original sewing stations. Books are sewn on to their original boards where possible, but if the leather covers need replacing, Mr Topping will visit the suppliers to look for a perfect match. Although he is surrounded by them, he admits to reading few books: 'When I was being trained at the British Museum, I was told to repair the books, not read them, or I would never get any work done.'

A PARCHMENT BOOK LOST IN THE THAMES was recently recovered completely intact. 'Water simply strengthens parchment, unlike paper. That is why several books have survived for more than 1,000 years,' says Wim Visscher, whose family has been making parchment and vellum since 1860. Using calf, goat and sheep skins, they cure the hides in the same way as leather. The hides are then dried and stretched on a frame so that they 'even out'. The cleaning process

Parchment Maker

involves scraping the skin down with a specialist 'lunar' knife with an 18-inch curved blade. The whole process takes about four weeks, during which time the skins are able to mature.

Mr Visscher's great-grandfather supplied parchment primarily for legal documents, but today clients include calligraphers, bookbinders, interior designers and the College of Arms. A one-off project involved restoration of the Domesday Book. 'The hinges on the book had damaged the parchment. We supplied strips as replacements on nearly every page. The type of parchment was exactly the same as we make now. Little has changed in 900 years.'

Mr Visscher is proud to inherit a skill that has been passed down by word of mouth through the ages and, with two daughters, three nephews and a niece, he is confident that the next generation will continue the craft. 'There will always be a need for parchment, because of its longevity. It is lucky the Dead Sea Scrolls were not written on paper.'

POTTERY MAY SEEM AN UNUSUAL CAREER for a Cambridge graduate to adopt, but Jim Keeling did just that, when he founded Whichford Pottery, whose decorative and often enormous terracotta pots are housed in gardens such as Blenheim Palace. He heads a team of more than thirty staff, who use methods perfected in the nineteenth century.

Potter

Each pot is individually made by throwing or hand-moulding the blended local clays. 'Throwing is the hardest part,' Mr Keeling says. 'We develop our techniques all the time.' Before firing in the kilns – where the grey pots turn the true terracotta colour – pots are decorated, fettled, turned and finally dried on top of the kiln. The largest pots take up to six weeks to complete.

For more intricate designs, the pots are hand-pressed from a plaster of Paris mould. The pot is created by coiling and beating the clay into these moulds. Unlike a machine-pressed pot, much of the work is done after the pot is freed from the mould, allowing details of leaves and fruit to be added.

Some patterns – such as family crests – are specially ordered, but Mr Keeling is continually creating new designs. Most of his inspiration is gained from visits to other potteries and to museums throughout Europe. 'The pot has to be a utilitarian object, so there are constraints on the shape,' he admits. 'But the more skilled we become, the more daring we get.'

R OGER HULME never travels to New York without his rolled umbrella and bowler hat. 'The taxis stop automatically for me, and I find I am always well looked after in restaurants,' he says. Since 1953 Mr Hulme has worked as a hat maker for Christy & Co. in Stockport, Greater Manchester, which makes top hats and bowlers in the traditional way. 'We've kept the old skills going while other people have lost them. In the early 1930s there were twenty or thirty hat shops in this area, but they have almost all disappeared.'

Top-Hat Maker

Rabbit-fur fibres are sucked on to a 4-foot-high cone and then shrunk to a shape about 9 inches tall. Christy's unique method for stiffening bowler and top hats entails treating the felt with shellac, before stretching it over a block, heating it in a stove and then letting it cool. 'It's like setting a jelly,' says Mr Hulme, who claims he can distinguish a Christy top hat from its imitators at eighty paces. 'Ours look quite different. The brim is kicked up, not straight, and the crown has a slope on it.'

JOHN JAQUES'S STORY is not unlike one of the hundreds of games that his company has invented – Happy Families. The company has been handed down from father to son for the past two centuries, making it the oldest games and sports manufacturer in the world. Christopher Jaques heads the company with his elder brother John; his sons, Ben and Emmett, are salesmen, having completed a stint on the factory floor – woodturning, painting and spraying, polishing and cabinet making – as every young Jaques must do.

Games Maker

It is hard to think of a game that is not a John Jaques creation: Snap, Tiddlywinks, Ludo, Snakes and Ladders are all Jaques inspirations, as is croquet, which Christopher's great-grandfather introduced into England from Ireland in 1851. Today, the Jaques's inventing days are over. 'There is no scope for it. Our job is to consolidate what we have already done,' says Christopher, who also organizes croquet days for clients.

The company manufactures mainly wooden-based games, 'because we are essentially a woodworking factory', as well as all types of balls. 'The electronic age did not help us at all, but now people are becoming more nostalgic in their interests.'

WHEN PETER STOCKEN WAS COMMISSIONED to make a large, triptych-style puzzle he knew that the client was particularly good at jigsaws, so he threw in a few additional puzzle pieces to confuse him. After the client had finally put together the whole thing, he saw that the extra pieces, once assembled, read: 'Ho! Ho!'

Puzzle Maker

This is typical of Mr Stocken's sense of humour and shows, in part, why his puzzles are so singular. Each is intricate, hand-made and tailored to the individual, and is frequently complicated enough to faze the likes of Einstein. It is not uncommon for clients to return his three-dimensional puzzles, a home invention and a speciality of Mr Stocken's, defeated: 'They know that if they are really stuck, we will put them back together for them,' he explains.

Mr Stocken's mother taught him how to make puzzles, using a pedal-operated saw with only his eye to guide him. He has handed down the technique to his own brood. Three of his four children make flat puzzles and, between them, they have made around four million puzzle pieces. Each of the puzzles contains intricately carved shapes – an umbrella, a violin, a hound, a golfer, an initial, or whatever is of particular interest to the client. In the case of the three-dimensional puzzles, the entire object is custom-shaped for the client in designs as diverse as a set of bellows, a head, or a four-leaved clover, as commissioned for Baroness Thatcher in 1987.

IN THESE DAYS OF DESKTOP PUBLISHING, it seems strange to find someone still working with hot metal instead of computers. Yet Stan Lane's business, Gloucester Typesetting, which produces short-run, limited-edition books, is flourishing. He treats typesetting as an art form. To him, a page of type should be as pleasant to look at as a picture, with the spacing between every letter kept 'even and beautiful'. For those looking for high-class typography with a tradition of excellence, there is no one better to turn to.

Typographer

Mr Lane started in the business aged fifteen, inspired by an old John Bull children's printing set, which he was given when he was twelve. He uses monotype, as opposed to old-style newspaper linotype, machines. These cast single metal characters in a variety of typefaces and sizes at a rate of 150 letters a minute. 'The way these characters sit together is far superior to anything that new technology can achieve,' he says. Clearly others agree, for publications that he has worked on are kept in a number of institutions and museums, including the Victoria and Albert Museum and the Getty Library in California.

W HITE SPACE IS THE KEY to typography, believes Ian Mortimer, founder of I.M. Imprimit, a full-time private press that uses a hand press, setting texts by hand from foundry type individually inked with a hand-held roller. 'What makes or breaks it is the way you use the space round the letter forms.'

Lumbering nineteenth-century cast-iron presses crowd all three floors of his warehouse in Hackney, East London. His 'first baby' is his favourite: the *Printer* Albion hand press that he picked up for £25 in 1969, in an era when old hand presses were thrown out for scrap metal. After studying at the Slade School of Fine Art he had been 'painting, teaching – surviving', when he bought the Albion to print his own woodcuts. 'But with it came some type, so I began to experiment with text,' Mr Mortimer says. Now he specializes in limited editions of artists' original prints. He won the Felice Feliciano book design prize for his Ornamented Types, the first printing of a unique collection of wood-engraved alphabets from the 1820s.

I N THE WORLD OF SEAL MAKERS, millennia come and go. 'Take me back 2,000 years in a

time machine, put me in a workshop in China or Japan, and I could get a job immediately,'

Neil Oliver says. 'The techniques have stayed almost the same.'

He was once asked to copy the engraving on the pommel of King John's sword. 'I took

rubbings and an impress from the original, which was brought to my workshop under guard.'

When engraving a crest on to a signet ring, he dusts the surface *Seal Maker*

with a fine layer of powder and traces the figures in reverse using

a sharpened quill. Then he cuts out the design with one of the wooden-handled tools that he has

made by hand. 'Scorpers, gravers, bull-sticks, spit sticks; I may not use some of them for ten

years, but it is so satisfying when there is something special that needs doing and you have got

exactly the right tool for it.' He holds the ring steady in a slot cut from the cork of a giant bottle

of whisky – bought only for the cork, of course.

AN AVERSION TO BALLPOINT PENS is one of the side-effects of Roy Zeff's job running Penfriend, the company that has its showcase shop in Burlington Arcade, London. 'I could not believe it when I saw Prince William, who is left-handed like myself, signing the register at Eton with a ballpen.'

Fountain-Pen Repairer

According to Mr Zeff and his partner Peter Woolf, writing with a ballpoint turns handwriting into a squiggle, because it does not give you any control of the paper, whereas writing with a fountain pen adds character to writing, because it creates some friction with the paper. 'Anybody can write with a fountain pen as long as the nib point is correct, which is why we sit people down and watch them write to make sure we pick the right nib for them. I can grind a nib down to suit them,' Mr Zeff says, explaining how he tailors pens to suit customers. He can also repair almost any pen. 'Most of the pen manufacturers refer their customers to us because we carry the spare parts that they no longer produce.'

Patience, a good eye, a steady hand and 'great knowledge' are the skills Mr Zeff describes as being required for his job: 'There are so many types of pen-filling systems that you need a good memory for them.' And Mr Zeff is optimistic about the future of the fountain pen: 'People are using pens more and more.' Perhaps he will convert Prince William.

THEY MAY NOT KNOW IT, but HM The Queen and the Lord Mayor of London have something in common. They both own a penknife made by Stan Shaw, the last 'little mister' – independent penknife maker – working in Sheffield. The penknife, following a Sheffield tradition, would have been exchanged for a coin so that 'friendship is not broken'.

Mr Shaw has been making penknives 'and nothing else' since he was fourteen. Then there were *Penknife Cutler* hundreds of companies and individuals making knives, but eventually the increase in factory-made knives put them out of business. 'I still make them how I was taught,' Mr Shaw says. They are crafted by hand, using gold, silver, ivory and mother-of-pearl. Sometimes it takes a week to make six, 'depending on how many parts are inside the knife and what material it is made of. I make an exhibition knife, which has all the old blades in it: the sheep-foot blade used by farmers, the peach-pruner blade used for fruit, the fleam blade, which vets used to use, every one had a special purpose.'

WHEN WILLIAM FORBES was asked to stuff a pet poodle and turn it into a pyjama case, he gave his customer short shrift. 'I don't believe in interfering with nature,' he explains, his Scots accent deep and mellifluous. As an ex-gamekeeper on the Mar Lodge estate, nature and the countryside are the inspiration for his work as the country's only taxidermist holding a Royal Warrant of Appointment. Most of the trophies that he makes or restores are for guns, such as someone's first

Taxidermist

stag. He also receives work from abroad. 'This buffalo comes from Africa,' he says, referring to the largest trophy in his studio outside Braemar, near Aberdeen. In this case, the skin and the skull would have been delivered by post.

Mr Forbes dresses the skin down to a viable thickness and places it over a mould. The skill lies in not damaging the skin and making the creature look as true to life as possible. When it comes to stuffing salmon, however, he relies on his talent as an artist. How does he make the scales look life-like? 'I use my wife's nail varnish.'

C HARLIE GREGORY IS STILL WORKING for S. Allen and Co., Treemakers Ltd, four decades after answering an advertisement in the St Pancras Chronicle. He has reached retirement age, but has no intention of stopping. 'I love working in wood.' The trees and lasts are made for well-known companies such as John Lobb, Henry Maxwell & Co. Ltd and Horace Batten, and go into all types of shoes and riding boots, including all the jackboots for the Household Cavalry.

Boot-Tree Maker

As well as managing the workshop, Mr Gregory does all the bench-work, fitting the trees once the wood has been turned on the lathe by colleague and fellow Londoner David Burns. 'It is a case of trial and error,' he admits. 'The tree has to be an exact fit to ensure that there are no gaps or stretching.'

The trees are made of beech from Romania and former Yugoslavia. It is steam-dried so that it does not alter its shape. English beech is 'too hard and knotty' to give a perfect, smooth finish. 'I also find the colour of the beech we use much more attractive.' Some shoe trees are made from obeche, a West African wood, which is lightweight and suitable for shoes that have frequently to be carried in suitcases.

A CHANCE REMARK to a friend over a drink in a pub set John Jones off on his career as a bellows maker. He mentioned that he had repaired a pair of old bellows. The friend wanted some repaired too. That was in 1978. Now Mr Jones makes bellows and restores old pieces for people countrywide, from his thriving workshop at the back of his home in Wiltshire. Bellows come in six varieties – double bellows are his own special invention – and although Mr Jones is

Bellows Maker

entirely self-taught, he always makes sure that he uses the best materials: elm, which was the traditional wood used; extruded brass rod for the nozzles; top-grade English cowhide for the leather; and solid brass-headed nails. He uses old models to cut new patterns.

Bellows were first shown on the frieze of Tutankhamun's tomb in Egypt, but those that exist today generally date from the 1920s and 1930s. According to Mr Jones, most of his clients tend to believe that their own set of bellows is much older. 'They always say they have had them in the family for generations, but bellows used to be packed with newspapers, and from these you can date them.'

I F ARTHUR NASH had taken up a profession other than making brooms, he would have broken a family tradition of 300 years. Besides, as he says, 'When I was young, it was assumed that you would do whatever your father did, and mine made brooms.'

Broom Squire

Although he makes up to a hundred brushes a day, the whole process takes nearly a year. The materials – birch for the brush and hazel for the handle – are cut during the sap-free winter, then stacked for at least six months to allow them to dry out and season properly. Mr Nash has an agreement with the local foresters, which enables him to collect his materials round Tadley on the Hampshire/Berkshire border. 'They are happy to have it cleared because birch is like a weed, which swamps other plants and saplings,' he says.

When ready, the birch is pressed and bound together with galvanized wire. After the handle has been shaved, one end is pointed and jammed into the birch. The besom brooms are then tied into 'dozens' in preparation for sale. They are used mainly for sweeping leaves, grass and hedge trimmings, and customers include staff at Hampton Court Palace, Kew Gardens and Buckingham Palace.

Mr Nash hopes that his son will continue the family tradition, but admits that 'It is more difficult to make a living out of besom brooms these days.'

W HEN A HALF-MADE CASK comes out of the steam bell, the cooper has only sixty-five seconds in which to knock down the truss hoops encircling the wooden staves and bend the barrel into shape. 'That's how long the steam lasts,' explains Alastair Simms of Wadworth & Co. in Devizes, Wiltshire. 'If you get it wrong, you can't put the cask back through the steamer.'

Cooper

Mr Simms, one of the last brewery coopers in the country, learnt his trade as an apprentice for Theakston's brewery in Yorkshire, and went on to spend sixteen years there, mending and remaking oak casks. Since joining Wadsworth's, his main task has been to cut down the 18-gallon kilderkins and convert them into 9-gallon firkins.

'The lifespan of a new barrel is about sixty years,' he says. 'The art is to get the cask the right size, by eye, so that when it's finished, it doesn't leak.' These days, coopers use German or Polish oak. 'It needs to be slow-grown and straight-grained for durability – the casks will be rolled in and out of the brewery once a fortnight.'

M AKING HAZEL WOOD for the thatcher's trade is a time-consuming and back-breaking task. 'I once managed to rip the muscles out of my ribcage,' says Mike Reeves, a broch maker based in Norfolk, supplying most of East Anglia with his products.

Mr Reeves began his working life as a field officer in charge of conservation projects with Norfolk County Council. Much of his time was spent restoring a semi-derelict ancient woodland as a working

Broch Maker

coppice, and it was this that drew him to the centuries-old woodland craft of making broches, the hooped pegs used by thatchers to pin thatch down. He produces 1,600 a day. He makes his broches from hazel, which he cuts himself. 'Every piece of wood is different,' he says. 'The first rive [split] is down the middle of the wood. If you get that wrong, then you get everything else wrong. It takes five minutes to be shown the craft, then a lifetime to learn how to do it properly.'

Mr Reeves also makes liggers, the straight pole sections on thatch. He considers them to be his *pièce de résistance*. Everyone notices the splendid criss-cross pattern on the roof. 'To see a hundred of these dead-straight triangles, 4 feet long, ready to be tied up, gives me a marvellous feeling of pleasure.' His greatest joy, however, is to drive round the Norfolk and Suffolk countryside where the thatchers have worked. 'My spirit is with those houses for the next thirty or forty years.'

EIGHTY YEARS AGO there were 150 pearl workers in the West Midlands. Today there is one company left – George Hook & Co. of Smethwick, Birmingham. 'Our business has survived because we have diversified so much,' says George Hook, who is the grandson of the company's founder and still working at the age of

Pearl Worker

ninety-one. Most pearl workers made only buttons, but Mr Hook and his son and grandson, both also called George, manufacture mother-of-pearl jewellery, salt, mustard and pepper spoons, knife handles and buttons.

The company, established in the 1830s, has changed little. It supplies specialist hand-crafted pieces to museums and private individuals, including intricate replica mother-of-pearl buttons for Victorian doll costumes. The pearl comes from Western Australia. Some 550–650 lbs of shells are delivered each spring and will last the Hooks for a year. From this they can produce 600 plain buttons a day and 200 of the more complicated button designs.

Mr Hook junior says that he is still learning the craft, even after thirty years in the business. 'It is a labour-intensive and intricate business. But there is nothing so great as seeing something which is so beautiful and gives so much satisfaction to other people. I would much rather have that than the money.'

ALL THE MATERIALS that Peter Faulkener uses to make his boats are sustainable, hence his motto that he makes 'the greenest boats afloat'. He does everything himself, apart from 'kill and skin the beast'. Mr Faulkener is one of the

Coracle Maker

few remaining people in the country who make traditional hide and willow coracles. Most modern coracles, of which there are about eighteen different types, are manufactured from calico and ash wood.

'I enjoy getting involved in all the processes of making coracles, from going to the forest to gather hazel in winter, to managing and harvesting the willow beds. The only unpleasant thing I have to do is scrape the hide, which comes fresh from my local butcher.'

It takes about fifty hours to make a coracle. The hazel framework is bolted down to a bed, bent up and tied across like bows. The structure is left to dry for ten days, while the hides are cleaned and soaked in a salt bath to cure. 'I semi-dry them on a frame and then lash them on to the finished framework with a horse-hair cord. As it dries, the hide tightens like a big drum.' The boats are sold to enthusiasts in Britain and abroad. A local friend has also purchased one. 'Because we go on the river together, we are now known as Ratty and Mole.'

AFTER ONLY A FEW WEEKS of being appointed marshman for the Broads Authority in Norfolk, Eric Edwards considered packing in the job. 'It is hard work and very physical,' he explains. But that was in 1967, and today he still finds himself knee-deep in water during winter, spending months rhythmically mowing weeds with a scythe so that he can dry them and turn them into bundles for the thatching industry. He makes it look deceptively easy, but it is a skilled job, taking up to three years to learn.

Marshman

Mr Edwards now loves his profession with a passion, and laments that he is one of the few marshmen left. 'We have real problems attracting the young.' Conscious of this, he gives talks and lectures to children who visit the Broads. 'Who knows, if I am enthusiastic enough, just maybe one of them will return to love and care for this special place after I am gone.'

I T IS A CURIOUS FACT, but the man who supplies anglers with the Rolls-Royce of fishing rods does not care for fishing himself. He would much rather be caught reading or playing golf than catching trout. But Laurence Stanton is the undisputed king of split-cane rod craftsmen. He is the last remaining rod maker at the House of Hardy, in Alnwick, Northumberland, and has been employed making rods since the 1950s. 'It is a difficult trade,' he says. 'The rods are made from 12-foot bamboo poles, cut to length, split, shaped, glued and straightened. It requires considerable hand-to-eye co-ordination.'

Split-Cane Rod Maker

Cane rods have been out of fashion since the more lightweight and cost-effective fibres came into existence during the 1960s, however, there are still a dedicated few who prefer fishing with a natural material. They appreciate the beauty of a finely crafted rod and can afford the £700 or so required to purchase one.

Hardy's used to make 200–300 rods a week in its heyday – no mean feat, given that it takes about one week to make a single rod. Proud of its craftsmanship, the company still places 'Palakona' cane rods in pride of place at the front of its brochure, and Mr Stanton is equally proud to be producing them. He plans to retire during the next few years, but hopes to train an apprentice to take over his craft.

H UNTSMEN WHO TWANGED the strings of their bows on the way home from the forest were the inventors of the harp,' says James Munson, who has repaired and serviced harps since leaving the army in 1948. Most of the harps played in London orchestras have, at some stage, been wheeled into the workshop he set up in Camden with Alan Harbour in 1973. Both men had formerly worked for a harp maker in South Kensington.

Harpist

'Harps are not stable. They often get damaged when moved about. We had one which had been backed into by a lorry outside a theatre, and another with a hole in its case made by a fork-lift truck.' The section of a harp most frequently needing repair is the wooden piece across the top, known as the harmonic curve. 'It has to be that lovely shape to accommodate the differing lengths of the forty-seven strings, like a grand piano.' Mr Munson speaks affectionately of the joints and strings of a harp, but he has never played one. 'We are artists, not artistes,' he says. 'We are far more practical than musicians.'

NEARLY EVERY TIME Allan Barrett sits down to watch the news on television, he can admire some of his handiwork – that is if the House of Commons is on view. 'The blue wallpaper with the white Gothic lilies and red roses, which you can see in the committee rooms, is one of ours,' he explains.

Wallpaper Maker

Mr Barrett has been making historical wallpapers for John Perry wallpaper factory at Coles & Sons, Islington, London, for the past three decades. He joined the company aged fifteen, first working as a tierover boy, hanging up the paper to dry and mixing and spreading dyes for the block-printing machines. After two years a table became free for an apprenticeship and his career there was made. It is skilled, painstaking work. 'Once we received a scrap of paper in a snuffbox and we still managed to get a perfect match.'

Some of the print blocks are 200 years old. Many would be familiar to William Caxton. 'They are in much better condition than the newer ones, because in those days people knew how to use and season wood properly.'

Gallery

DURING THE four years that *Country Life* has been running its Living National Treasures series, the magazine has been indebted to the number of readers who have written in to tell us about their local Treasure. Suggestions have included a couple from Beedon in Berkshire who run a village store that has been serving the local community for 150 years, and a terrier breeder who is preserving a pure strain of Jack Russell. Other nominees have included a tea lady who, although not practising a particular craft, is helping to preserve a particularly English tradition. This gallery of Treasures shows that Britain still boasts a vast range of skilled people who are each in their own way contributing to the country's heritage.

Hawk-Furniture Maker

When Roger Upton first started making hawking hoods and gloves during the 1950s, he was the only man in the country doing so. Now there are more hawk-furniture makers, but he remains the most authoritative, specializing in quality, hand-stitched hawking gloves made of buckskin. He also makes driving gloves and harnesses, and on one occasion created a hunting hood for a cheetah.

Gin Noser

Hugh Williams is master distiller for United Distillers, manufacturers of Gordon's gin, a company whose distillation programme has remained unchanged since 1769. Mr Williams uses his organoleptic skills (employing the senses of taste and smell) to detect flaws in the distillation process and to train nosers for posts abroad. 'It's like riding a bicycle,' he says. 'The more you do it, the better you become.'

Tea-Towel Designer

Pat Albeck thinks of tea towels as 'wonderful rectangular shapes with which to express one's artistic ability'. Having studied textile design at Hull and the Royal College of Art, she now creates designs for leading stores throughout the world. Her motifs and designs have become the hallmark of the National Trust.

Ecclesiastical Embroiderer

Leonard Childs was taught to sew by his grandmother at the age of four. He received his first major commission while at theological college in Wells, Somerset, and his work is now seen in cathedrals throughout the world. The techniques that he uses are rare, with some of the stitches originating in the thirteenth and fourteenth centuries.

Umbrella Maker

Joe Irish and Irene Zeegan have worked since 1978 and 1979 respectively, for the umbrella, walking-stick and whip firm of James Smith & Sons, London, which was established in 1830. Often using original Victorian tools, Mr Irish fits the ribs and makes the runners and catches, while Mrs Zeegan sews the gores and caps to make the covers.

Cheese Maker

Robin Congdon changed from farming to cheese making in the 1950s. 'I taught myself, learning the hard way, and found I had a talent for it.' He now supplies leading stores such as Harrods and Marks & Spencer, and runs the Ticklemore Cheese Shop, Devon. Mr Congdon's forte is blue cheese.

Harness Maker

Craig Leary is a driving-harness maker whose expertise lies in collars. He started in London during the 1970s, when 'hardly anybody was making collars. I had to pull apart old collars and learn by trial and error'. The rise in popularity of competition driving has increased the demand, and Mr Leary now supplies collars to companies around the world.

Glass Engraver

Laurence Whistler, who was born in 1912, trained as an architect and was later lured into engraving. Guided by books, he revived an eighteenth-century Dutch technique known as point engraving. Since then he has helped to found the Guild of Glass Engravers and his numerous works have inspired followers to adopt his craft.

Rope Maker

Norman Chapman, rope maker since 1976 at W.R. Outhwaite & Sons, North Yorkshire, is something of a pioneer. He helped to invent the Outhwaite cleat, a method of finishing off the ends of the rope using moulded plastic. Coffin handles, halters and dog leads are just a few of the items in his expansive repertoire.

Sundial Maker

Peter Parkinson describes himself as an 'artist blacksmith'. He originally studied design at the Royal College of Art, but became interested in ironwork when he joined a blacksmith workshop. Though he can turn his hand to anything from mirrors to candle-holders, he has added a contemporary twist to a traditional craft by making sundials.

Horticultural-Show Manager

Mavis Sweetingham first visited the Chelsea Flower Show when she was thirteen. She is now in the powerful position of organizer for the entire event. 'Each Chelsea takes eighteen months to prepare,' she says. 'I try to cover as many aspects of horticulture as possible, and to make each year's show different from the last.'

Cricket-Bat Maker

Tim Keely started making cricket bats aged sixteen. He joined John Newbery, makers of traditional bats and suppliers to Lord's. He took over the business when Mr Newbery died in 1989. All his bats are hand-made, using traditional tools and English willow. 'There is nothing nicer than watching cricketers using my bats,' says Mr Keely.

Fish Smoker

George Jackson settled in North Uist in the Outer Hebrides in 1969. Eight years later he started smoking salmon, using the local fuel, peat. He asked a friend in the trade for help and, together with his wife Rosemary, is now established worldwide. Choosing the right fish is the key to producing the best smoked salmon, he believes.

Gardener

Kenneth Littler and Thomas Acton have between them gardened at Arley Hall, Cheshire, for almost a hundred years. Mr Littler took on a tradition begun by his great-grandfather and is responsible for all the topiary work. Mr Acton, who has retired since this photograph was taken, joined at the age of fourteen and worked with Viscountess Ashbrook, the present hall-owner's mother.

Gun-Case Maker

Paul Margan is the leading maker and restorer of traditional oak and leather gun cases. All the cases are hand-stitched and take from a week to ten days to complete. He also makes tooled and stitched cartridge belts, gun slips and other items of leather work for shooting.

Groundsman

John Ponton is responsible for maintaining the immaculate croquet lawns at the Hurlingham Club in London. They are unrivalled anywhere in the world. Attracted to work in the open air, he joined the club in 1960. He sees a love of greenkeeping as the most important criterion. 'It's not a job you become wealthy at.'

Poultry Breeder

Will Burdett has spent a lifetime handling chickens. His particular passion is for Orpingtons. He says that his skill at handling these chickens is in his genes; his family has been breeding Orpingtons since the turn of the century. Once president of the Poultry Club of Great Britain, Mr Burdett was asked to take over the Queen Mother's flock. Under his care, it has won many prizes.

Silent-Film Pianist

Ena Baga, born in 1906, is the doyenne of silent-film pianists. Her father had one of the first cinema orchestras and indoctrinated Miss Baga and her three sisters in the art of silent films. She is confident that the appeal of such films will remain strong: 'They are about nostalgia. They will never be deserted.'

Stationery Engraver

Father-and-son team George and John Timms are masters in their craft of stationery engraving, working for Smythson of Bond Street. The elder Mr Timms began his career in 1937. He engraves the stationery, while his son prints it.

Grotto Builder

Diana Reynell used to teach jewellery design, but now she designs and restores grottoes throughout Britain and abroad. 'I have always been intrigued by caves and grottoes,' she explains. Her role is particularly appropriate, for many of the grottoes in Britain were originally built by women.

Breeches Maker

Michael Smith joined Bernard Weatherill of Savile Row as an apprentice breeches maker when he was fifteen years old. His clients range from HM The Queen to boxer Chris Eubank. The most popular fabric is wool, and a hand-made pair of breeches can cost up to £600.

Barometer Specialist

Patrick Marney restores and makes copies of antique mercury barometers. He combines the skills of a glass blower with those of a french polisher. 'It is a labour-intensive job,' he explains. His business has now moved from London to Melford Hall, Suffolk, where he works under National Trust patronage.

Butcher

To describe father-and-son team Gordon and Danny Hepburn simply as butchers would be doing them an injustice. Their shop supplies cheeses, wines and home-cooked produce, as well as meat. They are sole agents for Highgrove, HRH The Prince of Wales's estate. The business was founded in 1932 by Danny's great-grandparents.

Whisky Brewer

Hector Gatt is head brewer for Springbank malt whisky. Together with his staff of twenty-eight, he is responsible for maintaining the reputation of Springbank as one of the most complex and smooth malts in the world. Springbank, on the Mull of Kintyre off Scotland's west coast, is the only remaining distillery that is 100 per cent family-owned.

Heraldic Sculptor

Ian Brennan makes all the crests for newly appointed knights and members of the Royal Family. Working mainly in bronze and wood, he started as a heraldic sculptor in 1984. After a member of the Royal Household saw his work as a wildlife sculptor, he was approached to take on commissions for the Order of the Garter and the Order of the Bath .

Sausage Maker

Ryan Human works for Musk's delicatessen in Newmarket, Suffolk. He started his apprentice-ship at fifteen in 1959. Like his father before him, he keeps secret the recipe, established in 1884, for making the renowned sausages. Until 1979 the recipe was not even written down, but was passed from generation to generation by word of mouth.

Hooker Builder

Thanks to the Galway Hooker Association and to traditional builders such as Colm Mulkerrins, the fortunes of the Galway hooker have survived. The hooker is a single-masted working sailing boat, unique to the west of Ireland, and has been used for fishing and trading for 200 years. By 1970 the working fleet had been reduced to just two boats.

Posy Maker

Valerie Bennett-Levy is the official nosegay supplier to HM The Queen. Mrs Bennett-Levy, who was awarded an MVO in 1989, is by tradition a sculptor and painter. She became involved in making nosegays through her husband, who worked for a herbalist's. Traditionally posies were used to ward off illness and infection. Today they are simply a fragrant memento used for the Royal Maundy Thursday service.

Hedgelayer

Peter Tunks calls himself an agricultural contractor, but his forte is hedgelaying. Supreme champion at the national hedgelaying championships in Gaydon, Warwickshire in 1993, he has also won the South of England style competition eight times in a row. He started hedgelaying in 1963, aged seventeen.

Ribbon Worker

Maureen Brown is the longest-serving member of staff at Spink & Son, which has been manufacturing medals for the British Empire since the 1880s. She is responsible for the thousands of ribbons stocked at the factory. HRH The Prince of Wales frequently sends the company sashes and medals needing urgent repair.

Miniaturist

Michael Pierce is one of the few remaining traditional silhouette portrait painters. Card is the medium he uses most frequently, but he also paints on glass and plaster, using black ink overlayed with gouache. He started in 1980, having learnt his craft as a child from a profilist who had practised in Victorian London.

Millstone Dresser

Malcolm Cooper travels from mill to mill, redressing grinding stones, as stone dressers have done for centuries before him. The job involves chipping away at working surfaces, recutting furrows into millstones, stripping clean and repacking bearings on the millstone drive, and levelling the bottom stone.

Tanner

Raymond Purse joined Devon-based tanning company J. & F.J. Baker in 1949. He still works there, using a process almost unchanged since Roman times. A tanyard foreman for many years, he now concentrates on the currying or dressing of the leather for belts and shoes. His father was also a tanner.

Artist in Glass

'Glass harmonics in colour' is the wonderful phrase that Patrick Reyntiens uses to describe his work. He views himself as a painter who just happens to use stained glass as a medium. His windows grace the world, and in 1976 he was awarded the OBE for services to the arts. He argues that working in glass requires a combination of 'accuracy, discipline, definition, repetition and fine art'.

Gypsy-Caravan Restorer

Peter Ingram is never short of work, even though traditional gypsy caravans are a rare sight these days. As well as carpentry and joinery, he undertakes carving, gilding and scrolling. He also owns the Romany Folklore Museum at his base in Selborne, Hampshire.

Basket Maker

Russell Rogers takes pride in keeping alive a tradition that can be traced back to the Stone Age. A member of the Worcestershire Guild of Designer Crafts and trained at the Birmingham Workshops for the Blind, Mr Rogers is an experienced basket maker who can turn his hand to anything from picnic hampers to hobby horses for morris-dancers.

Sawyer

Jeremy Nelson is one of the few remaining suppliers of reclaimed pitch-pine in Britain. His skills lie in selecting and matching the wood for the job. Mr Nelson is entirely self-taught and founded his business in the late 1970s. He is heralded for his work on the new Glyndebourne opera house.

Clog Maker

Nelson Bailey, who owns The Clogger at Galgate, near Lancaster, is entirely self-taught. He had the good fortune to be given a full set of genuine cloggers' tools and patterns found in a disused clog shop. Mr Nelson still makes the traditional pit-clog model, but also livens up some clogs for fashion use.

Plume Maker

Louis Chalmers runs The Plumery in Chiswick, London. He is the sole supplier of plumes to the Household Cavalry and to all the foot regiments. Mr Chalmers served his apprenticeship with the firm of Appleton Brothers. He now corners the market in plumes, supplying theatres and armies worldwide.

Polo-Stick Maker

Gregor Glue has developed a reputation for fixing and mending polo-sticks. Based at Cowdray Park, he is now the only remaining commercial polo-stick maker and mender in Britain. An ex-polo player, he started his business in 1989. He has also set up his own line of 'Glue sticks'.

Tartan Weaver

Sybil Bunyan works for one of the few remaining traditional tartan-weaving firms in the country, D.C. Dalgliesh of Selkirk. Having started in 1980, she is now senior weaver responsible for ensuring that not a thread of colour is out of place. The technique has remained unchanged since just after the Second World War.

Marbler

Christopher Rowlatt runs his own business, Christopher Marbling, and specializes in producing strong and brightly marbled paper, based on traditional designs. He supplies bookbinders, interior designers and picture framers, among others. Years of experience have made him one of the most talented marblers of today.

Coppicer

Since 1966 Bill Hogarth's headquarters have been a small hut in a wood in Cumbria. He began coppicing at the age of fourteen, alongside his father, who founded the family business in 1939. 'It took me a couple of years to pick up the basics,' he says, 'but essentially I'm learning all the time.'

Hand Stitcher

Gary Finedon plays a key role at the long-established firm of Edward Green, famed for its hand-made shoes and boots. He is responsible for the stitching, using a method that has become almost extinct in the shoe trade. The company, which was founded in 1891, also makes boots for the Household Cavalry.

Golf-Club Maker

Barry Kerr retired as a professional golfer in 1976 and formed his own company manufacturing reproductions of, and restoring, antique golf clubs and balls. Hickory Sticks is already a great success. 'All the people who work with me are time-served craftsmen,' he says, 'but I also take on apprentices.'

Gun Maker

David McKay Brown produced the first round-action gun bearing his name in 1976, nearly twenty years after he began his apprenticeship with the Glasgow company, Alex Martin Ltd. He has a team of craftsmen, and in 1991 Mr McKay Brown developed the first new Scottish over-and-under shotgun since 1988.

Cuirass and Helmet Maker

Ken Middleton makes cuirasses and helmets for Firmin and Sons, like his father and grandfather before him. The company is chief supplier to the Household Cavalry. Once Mr Middleton received a letter from an officer apologizing for being 'rather tied up' and unable to keep an appointment. The letter, written in 1991, was sent from somewhere near the Iraqi border.

Rolls-Royce Builder

Dennis Jones is responsible for the enduring symbol of the world's most famous motor car. He has been making Rolls-Royce radiator shells since 1969. On the back of each shell, just below the Spirit of Ecstasy mascot, is the monogram of the craftsman responsible. Mr Jones is identified by a 'DD'.

Glasshouse Maker

John Lawson is general manager of Alitex, a company responsible for designing and building between 100 and 150 private and commercial glasshouses every year. Mr Lawson joined Alitex in 1986 after studying agricultural engineering. All the glasshouses are built on a bespoke basis.

Yeoman Raven Master

David Cope has been Raven Master at the Tower of London since 1991 and a Yeoman Warder since 1983. Following a tradition that goes back more than 900 years, the former Royal Marine's duties include letting the ravens out of their cages in the morning and whistling to encourage them to fly back in the evening.

Jewel Setter

Father-and-son team David and Andy Basford have been working together since 1983 at English Art Works, a company that produces jewellery exclusively for Cartier. Andy had to complete a five-year apprenticeship under his father, who was responsible for preparing the crown for HRH The Prince of Wales at his investiture.

Vintage-Car Builder

Keith Revell built his first car in 1956 at the age of seventeen. He is now one of the most important craftsmen at A.B. Price Ltd, which copies and restores vintage cars. Mr Revell makes the timber for cars such as Bentleys, Jaguars and Mercedes. His skills range from woodwork, carpentry and joinery to cabinet making and wood machining.

Furniture Maker

Philip Boorman has been making chairs in eighteenth-century styles since 1983 His work can be seen in Hampton Court Palace. Making an authentic replica requires accuracy of construction and craftsmanship, and also use of the correct wood. 'All these factors make the chairs stand out from mass-produced reproductions.'

Secateur Repairer

Tony Clayton is vital in preserving the reputation for excellence of Burton McCall, a company that supplies the Rolls-Royce of gardening tools, Felco secateurs. Anyone who owns a pair of Felco secateurs can send them to Burton McCall for repair. Mr Clayton, who trained in Switzerland, where the secateurs are made, has nurtured around 3,715 pairs of them.

Fly-Tyer

These days most flies are imported from Africa and Taiwan. Frankie McPhillips is one of the few professional fly-dressers left. He has been tying flies since 1978 and describes fly-tying as an exact science. It takes three minutes to tie a trout fly, but up to two hours to dress a full-display salmon fly.

Miller

Piers Garnham bought Bartley Mill in Sussex in 1985, and currently makes more than seventy different varieties of 'bespoke' flour. Mr Garnham believes that there is a growing market for specialist breads, and supplies about a hundred independent bakeries. His father and grandfather were millers before him.

Stamp Artist

Ian Loe was commissioned by the Crown Agents to be their main wildlife stamp artist in 1976. He travels widely to research insects, animals and plants throughout Great Britain and the Commonwealth countries. 'It is important to get a life-like attitude into the work, so I need to sketch the real thing,' he says.

Snigger

Without George Read, the art of snigging – removing timber from forests using horse power – might have died out. He learnt the trade from his father and has in turn taught his son, Kevin. Horses are more efficient than heavy machinery in thickly wooded areas, as they can reach otherwise inaccessible areas. There is an increasing demand for a move away from machinery and a return to snigging.

Pub-Sign Painter

Ken Allen is one of the most prominent pub-sign painters left in Britain, as computers have turned this form of painting into a dying trade. Employed in 1981 by Palmers Brewery in Dorset, he learnt his craft from George Biles, who had painted signs for seventy years. Mr Allen believes in matching the image on the sign to the pub name.

Ladies' Taylor

By the age of five, Roy Allen knew that he wanted to be a tailor. Ten years later he found himself working at Hardy Amies. After serving a nine-year apprenticeship, he started making suits for the great ladies of the day, including members of the Royal Family. He has now set up on his own and his outfits – from suits to ballgowns – are the work of a master craftsman.

Weaver

John McAtasney is weaver in residence at the Irish Linen Centre, Lisburn. He is the last full-time, hand linen-weaver in the British Isles. He has in his day provided linen for some distinguished clients, including many members of the Royal Family. He plans to train an apprentice to continue the tradition.

Mascot Maker

Sir David Hughes, Bt, stepped in to rescue Lejeune, a company specializing in the manufacture of car mascots, in 1978. Founded in 1910, Lejeune still makes hand-finished mascots, often using the original moulds. Sir David, a former sculptor and heraldic worker, designs and makes the special commissions.

Paper Maker

Christine Laver-Gibbs is a leading figure in her field. She supplies paper for books, documents and maps for the British Library, the National Trust and the Royal Bindery at Windsor Castle, to name just a few. Hand-made paper is a rarity these days. She works with her husband at Griffen Mill in Somerset.

Canal Boatman

Today there are only half a dozen horse-drawn boats still working on Britain's canals. John Head looks after one of the longest-serving, the 67-foot by 10-foot *Kennet Valley*, drawn by Hannah and Boncella. The boat belongs to Bob and Jenny Butler, who have owned the Kennet Horse Boat Company since 1979.

Lord's Dinner Lady

Nancy Doyle's name is known to anyone involved with the Marylebone Cricket Club. As the dining-room manageress, Mrs Doyle runs the kitchen and is the life and soul of Lord's. Starting in 1961 as a temporary worker, she received an honorary MBE in 1994 for her services to cricket and cricketers.

Rocking-Horse Maker

Tom Cobley started his family business making rocking-horses in 1983, because of the disappointment he felt when he went to buy a rocking horse for his daughter. He developed his skills by copying Victorian rocking horses, and each model is hand-carved using horse hair and leather tack.

Bar Manager

Victor Gower served Turkish coffee to Winston Churchill in 1944, during his first week at the Savoy. Mr Gower has been the bar manager at Simpson's-in-the-Strand since 1988 and is now the Savoy Group's longest-serving employee. His experiences – he was once held at gunpoint – have made him a legend.

Master Bowyer

Alan Pritchard is one of the few full-time bowyers in Britain, supplying all the major guilds and clubs; he is also a national coach and ex-international competitor. His longbows are constructed of a softwood and backed with hickory wood. Man-made fibre is used for the string, 'because it is more consistent'.

Toffee Maker

Neil Boustead keeps the secrets of the Toffee Shop in Penrith close to his chest. The fudge recipe for which the shop is famous has never been revealed. 'We have made the fudge the same way for the past eighty years.' His clients have included Lord Lichfield and HRH The Duchess of Kent, and he also supplies Fortnum & Mason.

Duck Breeder

Richard Waller is the last breeder of pure Aylesbury ducks in the country; the same bloodstock has been kept by his family since 1775. He started working for his father at the age of fifteen and took over the business in 1979. Each year he raises 10,000 ducklings.

Handle Bender

As far as he knows, Eddie Miller is the last person in Britain to practise the traditional craft of bending wooden umbrella handles by hand. Employed by Swaine Adeney Brigg, he steams the pieces of cane, heats them by blow-torch and bends them, by hand, into the perfect curve. 'If you left your umbrella in someone's umbrella stand, you would definitely know which one was yours.'

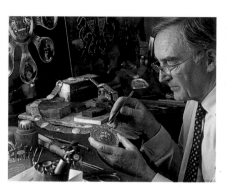

Ceremonial-Badge Maker

John Donald is a master craftsman of ceremonial badges of office, as well as a goldsmith and silversmith. Mr Donald studied at the Royal College of Art and worked as an industrial designer before opening his first jewellery workshop. He moved to his present Cheapside workshop in 1967.

Botanical Artist

Raymond Booth paints the plants and animals of his native Yorkshire. As one of the most highly regarded botanical artists in the country, his work is frequently exhibited at the Fine Arts Society in London and his paintings have also toured the United States. He has illustrated a book on Japanese plants and is presently mulling over another one.

Officer of Arms

In 1992 Elizabeth Roads was the first woman admitted to the ranks of the Officers of Arms as Pursuivant, at the Court of Lord Lyon in Scotland. 'We are derived from the heraldic messengers who used to carry out diplomatic missions abroad for the Crown,' she explains. 'I undertake ceremonial functions.' She also acts as Lyon Clerk and Keeper of the Records, dealing with correspondence and heraldic research.

Damascus-Barrel Maker

Paul Barber is the first man in Britain this century to produce new Damascus gun barrels. Mr Barber has worked in the gun trade since leaving school. He set up his own business in 1994 and has regular custom from a number of firms in the trade and from gun makers producing reproduction arms.

Silversmith

Royal silversmiths, BJS Company Ltd, revived the almost lost art of electroforming in the 1960s. Mike Cutts is in charge of BJS's project to electroform silverware for the restoration of the National Trust's Kedleston Hall in Derbyshire. 'Electroforming reproduces every scratch or bruise,' he explains, 'so it reveals the original character.'

Ice Sculptor

Duncan Hamilton is internationally acclaimed for his creations in ice for film sets, private parties and advertisements. He was introduced to ice sculpture while training to be a chef in London. Media coverage of his work elicited an avalanche of commissions. He now works in a studio in Wimbledon.

Rugby-Ball Maker

At the age of fifteen John Batchelor joined James Gilbert Ltd, boot and shoe makers for Rugby School, as an apprentice. He continues to make traditional rugby balls by hand, using cow hide with waxed threads. Inside the shop, founded in 1842, is the James Gilbert Rugby Football Museum; 14,000 visitors a year come to see the balls being made.

Mole Catcher

Jeff Nicholls believes he is one of the last professional mole catchers in Britain. He left school and tried a succession of jobs before finding his calling. Mr Nicholls realized that there was a market for mole catching when, one season, the Bracknell rugby pitch was plagued by molehills and he offered to help. To be a successful mole catcher 'you have to think like a mole', Mr Nicholls says.

Village Shopkeeper

Eleven days' holiday is all that Peter and Betty Pocock have taken since 1959, when they started running Purton Stores, in the Berkshire village of Beedon. Built as a farmhouse in 1598, the shop has now served the local community for a century and a half. Mr Pocock's father took it over in 1944 and it remains one of the few thriving village shops in the country.

Historical Cartographer

When John Garnons Williams looked up Shropshire in the Domesday Book, he noticed that the book, written in 1086, had no maps. It was not until 500 years later that maps were made of the British Isles. So he decided to tackle the task himself. He went on to make studies of medieval Scotland, Wales and Ireland, and now sells the maps at craft fairs and county shows, or by mail order.

Tram Superintendent

As tram superintendent, Michael Crellin has a job that is reminiscent of an age when horses were a natural part of people's working lives. At the beginning of every summer he and the first horse-drawn tram of the season set out along the Isle of Man's Douglas Promenade, continuing a tradition that – broken only by the Second World War – has endured since 1876. Mr Crellin breaks in and handles the horses himself.

Shell Artist

Peter Coke creates caskets, obelisks and sprays of exotic flowers in the style of Fabergé, from shells collected all over the world. A former actor and antique dealer, he sees his works of art as 'the antiques of the future'. But because his objects, regarded as collector's items, are made with a water-based glue, they are easy to break up – if future generations want to put the shells into their collections.

Slate River

Rex Barrow's father and grandfather were both quarrymen in the Lake District, as was his uncle, who taught him the trade when he was fifteen. Mr Barrow, born in 1935, has worked for Burlington Slate at Kirby-in-Furness since 1986; before that he did piecework at the many nearby quarries. The skill of a river is needed when the slate is split in half with a hammer and then split in half again.

Seat Weaver

John Hayward restores modern and antique chair backs and seats made of cane, rush and sea-grass, in a shop owned by his family for more than a century. He inherited the premises as a butchery business, but his hobby became a trade when he reopened the shop, selling cane and wooden crafts. Fans include Lord Montagu of Beaulieu.

Kite Maker

Nick Harrison is managing director of Brookite, a kite-making firm started by his grandfather in 1920. Some 200,000 brilliantly coloured kites are made each year in the converted corn mill that he shares with his wife, Mandy. He began making kites in 1969, taught by one of his grandfather's foremen.

Tassel Maker

Anna Crutchley hand-weaves tassels and fringes for upholstery and curtains, using only natural fibres. After studying textiles at art college, Ms Crutchley designed fabrics for a firm in Sri Lanka, and then returned to Cambridge to set up a weaving company, where she works to commission. It was she who wove the subtle trimmings in the Yellow Drawing Room at the Sir John Soane Museum, London.

Watch Maker

George Daniels remembers dreaming about watches as a child. He started a watch-repair business after leaving the army. He also wrote numerous books about watches. In 1969 he started making his own designs, producing about one watch a year. Every part of the watch is made by him, and each piece he produces becomes a collector's item.

Nurseryman

Terence Read is part of a family that has been growing and selling plants since 1750. With his wife Judy, and sons Simon and Stephen, he has developed Read's Nurseries, in the grounds of Hales Hall, near Norwich. He specializes in conservatory plants, including seventy-two different varieties of bougainvillaea.

Leather Worker

Bob Parry is chief leather worker for Connolly Leather, a family-run company established in 1878. He joined the company, whose leather has upholstered the benches in the Houses of Parliament, as an apprentice in 1958. He now works to commission, and projects have included replacement of the leather wall panels at Bawdsey Manor in Suffolk.

Food Historian

Peter Brears, a freelance food historian and museums consultant, is responsible for the revival of old, intriguing jelly recipes of the high Victorian period. He has held two jelly festivals at Harewood House, West Yorkshire. His jelly display showed the development of this dish from the fourteenth century. Mr Brears also advises on kitchen restoration.

Batman

Peter Cox is one of the most well-regarded helpers in the agricultural-show world. He has been senior batman at the Royal Bath and West of England Show since 1970. Born in 1932, he was introduced to the job by a friend who had been in service at the showground for thirty years. During the show he is on 24-hour call, with his day beginning at 4.30 a.m. when he makes tea and biscuits for the stewards.

Lavender Farmer

Henry Head became manager at his family's lavender farm, near King's Lynn in Norfolk, in about 1976. Now more than a hundred acres are cultivated, and the company was granted the Royal Warrant of Appointment to HRH the Prince of Wales in 1996. As with vintage wine, the finest lavender oil is the result of careful judgment and the right growing and harvesting conditions.

Terrier Breeder

Eddie Chapman is the owner of Britain's largest kennel of pure-bred Jack Russells – a distinct strain of fox terrier evolved by Jack Russell in Devon in the 1820s. His purpose is to preserve the breed, for he believes that it is 'on the brink of extinction' as a result of cross-breeding. 'I try not to have favourites,' he says. 'As with children, if you favour one, the others resent it.'

Fruit-Tree Trainer

Pat Marden has worked at Hatton Gardens, East Malling, Kent, since she left school. There she prunes and trains apple and pear trees planted in the 1930s, combining skills honed by tree trainers over the centuries with modern techniques. She is delighted with the innovation of electric secateurs: 'Far from ending up like a typist with a hand injury, I can continue tree development into the next millennium.'

Pondkeeper

Sidney McWilliams is one of Britain's few remaining village pondkeepers, having cast a custodial eye over Otford village pond in Kent for the past twenty-five years. Mac, as he is known, also looks after the duck house, which, like the pond, is a listed feature. 'We can have some unusual visitors,' he says. 'I once found a car submerged after a police chase.' Britain has lost more than a million ponds since the 1880s.

Tea Importer

When Lilian Prosser joined J. Atkinson and Company, tea and coffee suppliers in China Street, Lancaster, she was taught to weigh and wrap the different blends, labelling each quarter-pound package with the customer's name. That was in 1937, when tea was specially mixed. Today, Miss Prosser still works part-time for the business, which is jointly owned by Anne Riley, a member of the original Atkinson family, and Eric Thornton, who joined in 1954.

Bagpipe Maker

Piper and bagpipe maker Hamish Moore is a pioneer of the 1980s' revival of the eighteenth-century bellows-blown Scottish small pipes. As distinct from the more famous, mouth-blown Highland pipes, the small pipes are powered by bellows held under the arm. Mr Moore makes fifty sets of pipes a year and hopes that his two piper sons will take on his mantle.

Poppy Maker

Frank McNiff puts together more than 2,000 poppies a day at the Royal British Legion Poppy Factory at Richmond, Surrey. Mr McNiff, former farm manager, stuntman, merchant seaman and security officer, is one of 100 staff employed at the factory, which was established in 1922. Now holder of the royal warrant for manufacturing poppies, the Legion supplies the wreath laid by HM The Queen at the Remembrance Day service at the Cenotaph.

Brush Maker

The Robert Cresser brush shop in Edinburgh proudly claims to make 'a brush for every purpose'. Established in 1873, it is now owned and managed by Stephen Gilhooly, who started his employment there as an apprentice in 1970. Brooms and brushes are made from plane and beech wood, to which horsehair or Chinese wild-boar hair bristles are fixed. Some of the best-selling types have been stocked by the shop for half a century.

Hunt Tailor

Peter Ripley, of tailors Frank Hall of Market Harborough, Leicestershire, admits that he is part of a dying breed. 'There are no more than half a dozen hunt tailors across the country.' A major part of his job is to advise on the etiquette of hunting attire. Each coat is made up from 2–3 yards of 34-ounce cavalry twill, considerably tougher than the 10–12-ounce cloth used for normal suits, but not as heavy-duty as the material used a hundred years ago.

Kendal Mint-Cake Maker

Harry Wiper, great-great-nephew and last descendant of confectioner and inventor of Kendal Mint Cake, Joseph Wiper, was taught the recipe by his father at the family factory in Cumbria. A concoction of sugar, glucose and oil of peppermint, it is still made by Romneys in Kendal, and is renowned for its powers of providing energy without creating a thirst.

Stilton Maker

Sam Willder is the longest-serving employee at Long Clawson Dairy, one of the country's oldest manufacturers of Stilton. The cheese was traditionally made on local farms from surplus milk, but now it is in the hands of men like Mr Willder, who started in the trade at the age of fifteen. 'I learnt how to test the keeping-quality of raw milk – we used to take a sample in a ladle from a churn and test it with blue dye.'

Enamel Artist

Sue Pickford has played a significant part in reviving the Black Country town of Bilston as a leading centre for enamel production. She joined Bilston & Battersea Enamels, manufacturers of Halcyon Days enamels, in 1984 and is now premier artist at the company. A painter in her spare time, she says enamel painting is 'a totally different method from watercolours or oils. Some artists never master the technique'.

House of Lords Doorkeeper

Tact and understanding are important in Richard Skelton's profession as principal doorkeeper at the House of Lords. A visitor once asked him whether he could see Screaming Lord Sutch. 'He didn't believe me when I explained he wasn't a peer.' Mr Skelton is in charge of the twenty-two men who act on behalf of Black Rod, the Lords' official messenger, to ensure order in the House.

Mosaicist

The Albert Memorial, swimming pools, Underground stations and even bathrooms have all been worked on by the south-London-based artist Trevor Caley, who is one of a select few practising the art of creating and restoring mosaics. He likens his skill to that of a dentist: 'Cleaning old concrete off glass cubes is just like scraping plaque off teeth.'

Embroiderer

Anne Marie Butcher, embroider at the Royal School of Needlework based at Hampton Court, once made a coat for the Royal Regiment of Wales's mascot. 'Being a goat, it had eaten the previous coat we made for it.' She teaches a select group of apprentices that the school takes on each year, and repairs anything from altar frontals to teddy bears. She also pioneers modern embroidery designs, which are more fine art than craft.

Blade Cutter

Victor Ackrill admits that he is hopeless at gardening. 'If I put up a rose, it would turn into a thorn,' he jokes. But give him a dilapidated lawnmower and he will nurture it until it looks like new, for he can repair any machine, where others have failed before him. He fixes any small horticultural machine that has broken down, and he once worked on one that was originally intended to be horse-drawn.

Builder

Having spent nearly half a century in the business, Gilbert Larter is one of a few remaining builders who served a traditional apprenticeship, when apprentices were still being employed in the trade. 'I can turn my hand to most things,' he says. But his speciality these days is brickwork. 'I worry about the future. Without people being taught how to do things properly, standards in the building trade will be much poorer.'

Sheet-Metal Worker

Arthur Dutch uses the same set of Victorian tools that his grandfather did before him. Based in Edinburgh, Mr Dutch is the king of the tinsmiths, making reproduction lighting from his shop Lonsdale and Dutch. 'My grandfather went into business in 1921 with an American called Lonsdale, who returned to the States in 1922. Because the shop-front had been painted and stationery printed, it was a matter of economics that we didn't remove his name.'

Glass-Thermometer Blower

Ted Scott once constructed a thermometer that had to be made incorrectly to look right. 'It was for a film, so the thermometer had to show normal temperatures, even though it had hundreds of lights on it heating it up.' Mr Scott is used to challenges, however. Based at Russell Scientific Instruments in Norfolk, he is one of the few remaining experts on restoring antique thermometers and barometers using hand-blown techniques.

Wood Turner

Robin Wood is reviving a skill that disappeared in 1958 with the death of wood turner George Lailey. Mr Lailey was the only man in Britain to be practising the craft of wood turning using a foot-powered lathe to make wooden bowls. Mr Wood, whose previous career was in woodland conservation, has made replicas of all the old craftsman's tools. 'I use them to make plates and bowls based on traditional designs for museums and private individuals.'

Willow Merchant

Carlton Wright's father Jessie established the family business in 1895 after he met someone who was looking for willows suitable for making cricket bats. J.S. Wright & Sons has been a family concern ever since. Carlton, who is in his eighties, works alongside his nephew Nicholas and grandson Jeremy. They use specially cultivated willow, which is cleaved and cut into lengths before it is shipped to bat makers all around the world.

Ornamenter

Brian Bates is the third generation of his family to have been employed by Wedgwood as an ornamenter in what is known as 'prestige'. This is the section where the most expensive Wedgwood products, namely the famous blue and white jasper clays, are produced. Mr Bates, who has been with the company for thirty-five years, reveals, 'All the clay is a pinkish colour at the outset. It is not until it is fired that it changes colour.'

Mount Cutter

Sarah Spicer designs and cuts by hand card-mounts for period watercolours, paintings, drawings and prints. She executes hand-painted washes or coloured lines in the historic style appropriate to the period of the painting or drawing. She works from a seventeenth-century country house in Suffolk, and has designed and cut mounts for private collectors in Britain and abroad, as well as for institutions such as the Sir John Soane Museum.

Bait Digger

Each winter, dressed in layers of clothes to ward off the cold, Duncan Groom digs for lugworms as his father did for many years before him. The prime bait for cod anglers, lugworms lie some 18 inches below the sand on long stretches of beach along the Norfolk coast-line. They used to be caught in their thousands, but nowadays Mr Groom says he collects an average of 500 each outing. 'They are going, and we diggers have almost gone too.'

Coach Painter

Septuagenarian Russell Bampton has a hand still steady enough to paint intricate lines on carriages, pony traps and vintage cars using a fine ox-hair and sable brush, which he makes himself. 'It means I can do the fine lines properly,' he says. Mr Bampton has been practising his trade for more than fifty years and has painted vintage cars for the National Museum and the electric vans used by Harrods. It can take up to three months to complete the work.

Addresses

ARCHITECTURAL
DRAUGHTSMAN
Eric Throssell
19 St Mary's Square
Aylesbury
Buckinghamshire HP20 2JJ
01296 415435

ARTIST IN GLASS
Patrick Reyntiens
Ilford Bridges Farm
Close Stocklinch
Ilminster
Somerset TA19 9HZ
01460 52241

BAGPIPE MAKER
Hamish Moore
St Mary's Road
Birnam
Perthshire PH8 0PJ
01738 444554

BAIT DIGGER
Duncan Groom
106 High Street
Blakeney
Norfolk NR25 7NX

BAR MANAGER
Victor Gower
c/o Simpson's-in-the-Strand
100 The Strand
London WC2R 0EW
0171 836 9112

BAROMETER SPECIALIST
Patrick Marney
The Gate House
Melford Hall
Long Melford
Sudbury
Suffolk CO10 9AA
01787 880533

BASKET MAKER
Russell Rogers
The Basket Maker
Main Street
South Littleton
Evesham
Worcestershire WR11 5TJ
01386 830504

BATMAN
Peter Cox
c/o Royal Bath and West of
England Society
The Showground
Shepton Mallet
Somerset BA4 6QN
01749 822200

BELL FOUNDER
Danny Matholus
Whitechapel Bell Foundry
34 Whitechapel Road
London E1 1DY
Fax: 0171 375 1979

BELLOWS MAKER
John Jones
35 Milton Lilbourne
Near Pewsey
Wiltshire SN9 5LQ
01672 562696

BLADE CUTTER
Victor Ackrill
Elvic of Louth
Cinder Lane
Louth
Lincolnshire LN11 9HS
01507 602680

BOILER MAKER
Robert Bicknell
A.G. Bicknell & Co.
Hollycombe Steam Collection
Hollycombe
Liphook
Hampshire GU30 7LP
01428 725094

BOOKBINDER
Bill Topping
Lambeth Palace Library
London SE1 7JU
0171 928 6222

BOOT-TREE MAKER
Charlie Gregory
S. Allan and Co.
37 Gosfield Street
London W1P 7HA
0171 636 2611

BOTANICAL ARTIST
Raymond Booth
22 Far Moss
Leeds LS17 7NR
01132 672003

BREECHES MAKER
Michael Smith
Bernard Weatherill Ltd
7/8 Savile Row
London W1X 1AS
0171 734 6905

BRICK MAKER
Bill Watkinson
Michelmersh Brick & Tile Co. Ltd
Hillview Road
Romsey
Hampshire SO51 0NN
01794 368506

BROCH MAKER
Mike Reeves
The Drifts
Oak Covert
Didlington
Thetford
Norfolk IP26 5AU
01842 878368

BRONZE FOUNDER
Ted Knell
Burghleighfield Arts Ltd
High Wycombe
Buckinghamshire HP10 9RF
01494 521341

BROOM SQUIRE
Arthur Nash
A. Nash Besom Brooms
46 Mulfords Hill
Tadley
Hampshire RG26 3JE

BRUSH MAKER
Stephen Gilhooly
Robert Cresser
40 Victoria Street
Edinburgh EH1 2JW
0131 225 2181

BUILDER
Gilbert Larter
Campana
Whympwell Street
Happysburgh
Norwich NR12 0QD
01692 650728

BUTCHER
Gordon and Danny Hepburn
Hepburns
269 Roman Road
Mountnessing
Nr Brentwood
Essex CM15 0UH
01277 353063

CANAL BOATMAN
John Head
Kennet Horse Boat Company
22 West Mills
Newbury
Berkshire RG14 5HU
01635 44154

CEREMONIAL-
BADGE MAKER
John Donald
120 Cheapside
London EC2V 6DR
0171 606 2675

CHEESE MAKER
Robin Congdon
Ticklemore Cheese Shop
1 Ticklemore Street
Totnes
Devon TQ9 5EJ
01803 865926

COACH PAINTER
Russell Bampton
89 Tremona Road
Shirley
Southampton SO1 6HU

COAT MAKER
Daniel Timmins and Keith Levett
Henry Poole & Co.
15 Savile Row
London W1X 1AE
0171 734 5985

COOPER
Alastair Simms
Wadworth & Co. Ltd
Northgate Brewery
Devizes
Wiltshire SN10 1JW
01380 723361

COPPICER
Bill Hogarth
Spark Bridge
Nr Ulverston
Cumbria LA12 7RS
01229 861513

CORACLE MAKER
Peter Faulkener
24 Watling Street
Leintwardine
Shropshire SY7 0LW
01547 540629

COUNTRY-HOUSE PAINTER
Jonathan Myles-Lea
Cefn Vaynor Chapel House
Berriew
Montgomeryshire SY21 8PW
01686 640470

CRICKET-BAT MAKER
Tim Keely
John Newbery Ltd
Station Road
Robertsbridge
East Sussex TN32 5DG
01580 881104

CUIRASS AND
HELMET MAKER
Ken Middleton
Firmin and Sons Plc
82/86 New Town Row
Birmingham B6 4HU
01213 596666

DAMASCUS-BARREL MAKER
Paul Barber
The Coach House
Moccas
Hereford HR2 9LE
01981 500634

DRYSTONE WALLER
George Hall
3 Drakestone View
Harbottle
Morpeth
Northumberland NE65 7DF
01669 650273

DUCK BREEDER
Richard Waller
Long Grove Wood Farm
234 Chartridge Lane
Chesham
Buckinghamshire HP5 2SG
01494 772744

ECCLESIASTICAL
EMBROIDERER
Leonard Childs
St Mark's Vicarage
119 Francis Street
Derby DE21 6DE
01332 340183

EMBROIDERER
Anne Marie Butcher
Hampton Court Palace
Surrey KT8 9AU
0181 781 9500

ENAMEL ARTIST
Sue Pickford
c/o Halcyon Days
14 Brook Street
London W1Y 1AA
0171 629 8811

FARRIER
Bernard Tidmarsh
Ye Olde Forge
Tetbury Lane
Crudwell
Malmesbury
Wiltshire SN16 9HE
01666 577665

FISH SMOKER
George and Rosemary Jackson
Mermaid Fish Supplies
Clachan
Lochmaddy
North Uist
Outer Hebrides HS6 5HD
01876 580209

FOOD HISTORIAN
Peter Brears
4 Woodbine Terrace
Headingley
Leeds LS6 4AF
01132 756537

FOUNTAIN-PEN REPAIRER
Roy Zeff
Penfriend (Burlington) Ltd
34 Burlington Arcade
Piccadilly
London W1V 9AD
0171 499 6337

FREEMINER
Ray and Jonathan Wright
Clearwell Caves
Nr Coleford
Royal Forest of Dean
Gloucestershire GL16 8JR
01594 832535

FRUIT-TREE TRAINER
Pat Marden
Horticulture Research
International
East Malling
Nr West Malling
Kent ME19 6BJ
01732 843833

FURNITURE MAKER
Philip Boorman
Philip Boorman Furniture Ltd
Slater Street
High Wycombe
Buckinghamshire HP13 6ES
01494 530777

GAMES MAKER
The Jaques Family
John Jaques Croquet
361 Whitehorse Road
Thornton Heath
Surrey CR7 8XP
0181 684 4242

GARDENER
Kenneth Littler & Thomas Acton
Arley Hall and Gardens
Arley
Northwich
Cheshire CW9 6NA
01565 777353

GILDER AND CARVER
Christine Palmer
Carvers & Gilders
9 Charterhouse Works
Eltringham Street
London SW18 1TD
0181 870 7047

GIN NOSER
Hugh Williams
United Distillers Plc
Fenton Way
Laindon
Basildon
Essex SS15 6SH
01268 544001

GLASS ENGRAVER
Laurence Whistler
Scriber's Cottage
High Street
Watlington
Oxford OX9 5PY
01491 612591

GLASSHOUSE MAKER
John Lawson
Alitex Ltd
Station Road
Alton
Hampshire GU34 2PZ
01420 82860

GLASS-THERMOMETER
BLOWER
Ted Scott
Russell Scientific Instruments Ltd
Rash's Green Industrial Estate
East Dereham
Norfolk NR19 1JG
01362 693481

GOLF-CLUB MAKER
Barry Kerr
Heritage Golf of St Andrews Ltd
Argyle Business Park
Largo Road
St Andrews
Fife KY16 8PG
01334 477299

GROTTO BUILDER
Diana Reynell
13 Fournier Street
London E1 6QE
01432 359203

GROUNDSMAN
John Ponton
c/o The Hurlingham Club
Ranelagh Gardens
London SW6 3PR
0171 736 8411

GUN-CASE MAKER
Paul Margan
Just So Cottage
11 The Walk
Winslow
Buckinghamshire MK18 3AJ
01296 714548

GUN MAKER
David McKay Brown
32 Hamilton Road
Bothwell
Glasgow G71 8NA
01698 853727

GYPSY-CARAVAN RESTORER
Peter Ingram
Romany Folklore Museum
Selborne
Hampshire GU34 3JW
01420 511486

HAND STITCHER
Gary Finedon
Edward Green & Co
The Chelsea Workshops
74/76 Cowper Street
Northampton NN1 3QR
01604 713199

HANDLE BENDER
Eddie Miller
Swaine Adeney Brigg Ltd
Nursery Road
Great Chesterford
Essex CB10 1QW
01799 530521

HARNESS MAKER
Craig Leary
31 Greenwich
Fonthill
Gifford
Tisbury
Nr Salisbury
Wiltshire SP3 6QL

HARPIST
James Munson
Munson & Harbour
Masterpiece Works
Hampshire Street
London NW5 2TE
0171 267 1610

HAWK-FURNITURE MAKER
Roger Upton
Plough Cottage
The Bath Road
Marlborough
Wiltshire SN8 1PT
01672 861656

HAY-RAKE MAKER
John Rudd
The Sawmills
Dufton
Appleby
Cumbria CA16 6DD

HEDGELAYER
Peter Tunks
The Coach House
Warltersville
Way
Horley
Surrey RH6 9EP
01293 784826

HERALDIC SCULPTOR
Ian Brennan
21 Hornby Close
Warsash
Nr Southampton SO31 9GN
01489 574782

HISTORICAL
CARTOGRAPHER
John Garnons Williams
GWP
PO Box 274
Shrewsbury SY4 4WA
01939 210416

HOOKER BUILDER
Colm Mulkerrins
Mynish Carna
County Galway
Irish Republic
00353 9532327

HORTICULTURAL-SHOW
MANAGER
Mavis Sweetingham
Royal Horticultural Society
Vincent House
80 Vincent Square
London SW1P 2PE
0171 834 4333

HOUSE OF LORDS
DOORKEEPER
Richard Skelton
House of Lords
London SW1A 0PW
0171 219 3000

HUNTSMAN
Bruce Durno
Fernie Hunt Kennels
Great Bowden
Market Harborough
Leicestershire LE16 7HS
01858 465372

HUNT TAILOR
Peter Ripley
Frank Hall
30 St Mary's Road
Market Harborough
Leicestershire LE16 7DU
01858 462412

ICE SCULPTOR
Duncan Hamilton
5 Lampton House Close
Wimbledon
London SW19 5EX
0181 944 9787

JEWEL SETTER
David and Andy Basford
English Art Works
105/106 New Bond Street
London W1Y 9LG
0171 408 5754

KENDAL MINT-CAKE MAKER
Harry Wiper
44 Burneside Road
Kendal
Cumbria LA9 4RL
01539 728883

KITE MAKER
Nick and Mandy Harrison
Brookite
Brightley Mill
Okehampton
Devon EX20 1RR
01837 53315

LADIES' TAILOR
Roy Allen
34 Ashchurch Grove
London W12 9BU
0181 743 3331

LAVENDER FARMER
Henry Head
Norfolk Lavender Ltd
Caley Mill
Heacham
Kings Lynn
Norfolk PE31 7JE
01485 570384

LEATHER WORKER
Bob Parry
Connolly Ltd
32 Grosvenor Crescent Mews
London SW1X 7EX
0171 235 3883

LORD'S DINNER LADY
Nancy Doyle
c/o Marylebone Cricket Club
Lord's Cricket Ground
St John's Wood
London NW8 8QN
0171 289 1611

MARBLER
Christopher Rowlatt
14 Hereford Street
Presteigne
Powys
Wales LD8 2AR
01544 260466

MARSHMAN
Eric Edwards
c/o Broads Authority
18 Colegate
Norwich
Norfolk NR3 1BQ
01603 610734

MASCOT MAKER
Sir David Hughes, Bt, MA
Louis Lejeune Ltd
The Berristead
Wilburton
Ely
Cambridgeshire CB6 3RP
01353 740444

MASTER BOWYER
Alan Pritchard
72 Oldfield Road
Chapelfields
Coventry CV5 8FW
01203 672846

MILLSTONE DRESSER
Malcolm Cooper
Carom Water Crafts
365 Snarlton Lane
Melksham
Wiltshire SN12 7QW
01225 707153

MINIATURIST
Michael Pierce
10 St Peter's
West Street
Chichester
West Sussex PO19 1QU
01243 784453

MOLE CATCHER
Jeff Nicholls
Bracknell Pest Control Ltd
2 Talbot Cottages
Forest Road
Wokingham
Berkshire RG40 5SG

MOSAICIST
Trevor Caley
Trevor Caley Associates Ltd
17 High Street
Stock, Ingatestone
Essex CM4 9BD
01277 840101

MOUNT CUTTER
Sarah Spicer
01359 230 349

NAIL MAKER
Rupert Rea
c/o Avoncroft Museum
Stoke Heath
Bromsgrove
Worcestershire B60 4JR
01527 831886

NURSERYMAN
Terence Read
Read's Nurseries
Hales Hall, Loddon
Nr Norwich
Norfolk NR14 6QW
01508 548395

OFFICER OF ARMS
Elizabeth Roads
Court of the Lord Lyon
HM New Register House
Edinburgh EH1 3YT
0131 556 7255

ORNAMENTOR
Brian Bates
Wedgwood
Barlaston
Stoke-on-Trent ST12 9ES
01782 204141

PAPER MAKER
Michael and Christine Laver-Gibbs
Griffem Mill
The Old Mill
Croscombe
Nr Wells
Somerset BA5 3QN
01749 330117

PARCHMENT MAKER
Wim Visscher
97 Caldecote Street
Newport Pagnell
Buckinghamshire MK16 0DB
01908 610038

PEARL WORKER
George Hook
George Hook & Co.
Corner Building
Pope Street
Smethwick
West Midlands B66 2JP
0121 558 2186

PENKNIFE CUTLER
Stan Shaw
6 St Matthias Road
Deepcar
Sheffield S30 5SG
01142 883996

PLASTERER
Leonard Grandison
L. Grandison & Son
Innerleithen Road
Peebles EH45 8BA
01721 720212

PLOUGHMAN
Jack House
The Dairy Farm
Quidhampton
Wilton
Wiltshire

PLUME MAKER
Louis Chalmers
16 Deans Close
Whitehall Gardens
Chiswick W4 3LX
0181 995 7099

POLO-STICK MAKER
Gregor Glue
The Polo Splice
126 Litte Todham
Midhurst
West Sussex GU29 0BU
01730 814991

PONDKEEPER
Sidney Albert McWilliams
6 High Street
Otford
Nr Sevenoaks
Kent TN14 5PQ
01959 522150

POPPY MAKER
Frank McNiff
The Royal British Legion Poppy
Factory Ltd
20 Petersham Road
Richmond
Surrey TW10 6UR
0181 940 3305

POSY MAKER
Valerie Bennett-Levy
Malvern
Highfield Crescent
Hindhead
Surrey GU26 7TG
01428 604853

POTTER
Jim Keeling
Whichford Pottery
Whichford
Nr Shipston-on-Stour
Warwickshire CV36 5PG
01608 684416

POULTRY BREEDER
Will Burdett
The Laurels
Hutton Sessay
Thirsk
North Yorkshire YO7 3BA
01845 501256

PRINTER
Ian Mortimer
I.M. Imprimit
219a Victoria Park Road
London E9 7HD
0181 986 4201

PUB-SIGN PAINTER
Ken Allen
J.C. & R.H. Palmer Ltd
The Old Brewery
West Bay Road
Bridport
Dorset DT6 4JA
01308 422396

PUZZLE MAKER
Peter Stocken
Puzzleplex
Stubbs Common Farm
Stubbs Walden
Doncaster
South Yorkshire DN6 9BU
01302 700997

RARE-PLANT CONSERVATOR
Elizabeth Braimbridge
Langley Boxwood Nursery
Rake
Nr Liss
Hampshire GU33 7JL
01730 894467

RIBBON WORKER
Maureen Brown
c/o Spink & Son
5 King Street
St James's
London SW1Y 6QS
0171 930 7888

RIDING-HAT MAKER
Ray Corne
Patey London Ltd
1 Amelia Street
London SE17 3PY
0171 703 6528

RIGGER
Keith Garnett
The Rope House
39a Wheatash Road
Addlestone
Surrey KT15 2ES
01932 561355

ROCKING-HORSE MAKER
Tom Cobley
Whiddecombe Cottage
Pond Lane
Greetham
Oakham
Rutland LE15 7NW
01572 812800

ROLLS-ROYCE BUILDER
Dennis Jones
c/o Rolls-Royce Motorcars Ltd
Crewe
Cheshire CW1 3PL
01270 255155

ROPE MAKER
Norman Chapman
W.R. Outhwaite & Son
Town Foot
Hawes
North Yorkshire DL8 3NT
01969 667487

ROSETTE MAKER
Frank West
The PO Workshop
Dark Lane
Sherborne St John
Basingstoke
Hampshire RG24 9HR
01256 850857

RUGBY-BALL MAKER
John Batchelor
James Gilbert Rugby Footballs Ltd
5 St Matthews Street
Rugby CV21 3BY
01788 542426

RUSTIC-HUT MAKER
David and Andrew Raffle
Raffles
Church Farm
Main Street
Overseal
South Derbyshire DE12 6LG
01283 762469

SADDLER
S. Milner & Son
Unit 4
Rural Industries
John O'Gaunt
Melton Mowbray
Leicestershire LE14 2RE
01664 454839

SAUSAGE MAKER
Ryan Human
Musk's Ltd
Unit 4
Goodwin Business Park
Willie Snaith Road
Newmarket
Suffolk CB8 7SQ
01638 662626

SEAL MAKER
Neil Oliver
Logie Steading
Forres
Moray IV36 0QN
01309 611255

SEAT WEAVER
John Hayward
Cane and Woodcraft Centre
57 High Street
Beaulieu
Hampshire SO42 7YA
01590 612211

SECATEUR REPAIRER
Tony Clayton
Burton McCall Ltd
163 Parker Drive
Leicester LE4 0JP
0116 2340800

SHEET- METAL WORKER
Arthur Dutch
Lonsdale & Dutch
23b Howe Street
Edinburgh EH3 6TF
0131 556 3257

SHELL ARTIST
Peter Coke
c/o The O'Shea Gallery
120a Mount Street
London W1Y 5HB
0171 629 1122

SILENT-FILM PIANIST
Ena Baga
c/o Heather Osborn
Programme Planning
National Film Theatre
South Bank
Waterloo
London SE1 8XT
0171 815 1311

SILVERSMITH
Mike Cutts
BJS Company Ltd
65 Bideford Avenue
Perivale
Greenford
Middlesex UB6 7PP
0181 810 5779

SLATE RIVER
Rex Barrow
Burlington Slate Ltd
Cavendish House
Kirkby-in-Furness
Cumbria LA17 7UN
01229 889661

SNIGGER
George Read
3 Church Road
Witherslack
Grangeover Sands
Cumbria LA11 6RP
01539 552481

SPLIT-CANE ROD MAKER
Laurence Stanton
c/o House of Hardy
Willowburn
Alnwick
Northumberland NE66 2PF
01665 602771

STAMP ARTIST
Ian Loe
7 The Manor
Potton
Sandy
Bedfordshire SG19 2RN
01767 261516

STATIONERY ENGRAVER
George & John Timms
c/o Frank Smythson
40 New Bond Street
London W1Y 0DE
0171 629 8558

STILTON MAKER
Sam Willder
Long Clawson Dairy Ltd
Long Clawson
Leicestershire LE14 4PJ
01664 822332

SUNDIAL MAKER
Peter Parkinson
Heathfield House
Shortheath Common
Oakhanger
Bordon
Hampshire GU35 9JT
01420 477191

TANNER
Raymond Purse
J and FJ Baker & Co. Ltd
The Tannery
King Street
Colyton
Devon EX13 6PD
01297 552282

TARTAN WEAVER
Sybil Bunyan
D.C. Dalgliesh Ltd
Dunsdale Mill
Selkirk TD7 5EB
01750 20781

TASSEL MAKER
Anna Crutchley
The Frater
6b Prairie Road
Cambridge CB5 8HT
01223 327685

TAXIDERMIST
William Forbes
Deeview Studio
Corriemulzie
Braemar
Aberdeenshire AB35 5YB
013397 41676

TEA IMPORTER
Lilian Prosser & Eric Thornton
J. Atkinson & Co.
China Street
Lancaster LA1 1EX
01524 65470

TEA-TOWEL DESIGNER
Pat Albeck
4 Western Terrace
London W6 9TX
0181 748 3990

TERRIER BREEDER
Eddie Chapman
Fox Warren Kennels
Vines Close Farm
Henbury
Nr. Wimborne
Dorset DH21 3RW
01258 857801

THATCHER
Frank Turbitt
Fourwinds
Ladram Road
Etterton
Nr Budleigh Salterton
Devon EX9 7HT
01395 568202

and: David Turbitt
Newlyn
Greenway Lane
Sidmouth
Devon EX10 0LZ
01395 514184

TOFFEE MAKER
Neil Boustead
The Toffee Shop
7 Brunswick Road
Penrith
Cumbria CA11 7LU
01768 862008

TOP-HAT MAKER
Roger Hulme
Christy & Co. Ltd
Higher Hillgate
Stockport
Cheshire SK1 3EU
0161 480 8731

TRAM SUPERINTENDENT
Michael Crellin
Douglas Corporation
Karrow Keil House
Patrick Road, St Johns
Isle of Man
IM4 3BM
01624 625076

TYPOGRAPHER
Stan Lane
Gloucester Typesetting Services
Unit 23e
Bonds Mill
Stonehouse
Gloucestershire GL10 3RG
01453 825623

UMBRELLA MAKER
Joe Irish and Irene Zeegan
James Smith & Sons Ltd
Hazlewood House
53 New Oxford Street
London WC1A 1BL
0171 836 4731

VILLAGE SHOPKEEPER
Peter and Betty Pocock
Purton Stores
Beedon
Nr Newbury
Berkshire RG20 8SN
01635 248408

VINTAGE-CAR BUILDER
Keith Revell
A.B. Price Ltd
Hardwick House
Studley
Warwickshire B80 7AF
01527 852377

WALLPAPER MAKER
Allan Barrett
Cole & Son Wallpaper Ltd
142/144 Offord Road
London N1 1NS
0171 607 4288

WATCH MAKER
Dr George Daniels
Riversdale
Lezayre
Isle of Man IM7 2EA
01624 814917

WEATHERMAN
Bill Foggitt
South Villa
York Road
Thirsk
North Yorkshire YO7 3AA
01845 522140

WEAVER
John McAtasney
c/o Irish Linen Centre and Lisburn
Museum
Market Square
Lisburn
County Antrim
Northern Ireland BT28 1AG
01846 663377

WHISKY BREWER
Hector Gatt
Springbank Distillery
Campbeltown
Argyll PA28 6ET
01586 552085

WIG MAKER
Kathleen Clifford
Ede & Ravenscroft
93 Chancery Lane
London WC2A 1DU
0171 405 3906

WILLOW MERCHANT
The Wright Family
J.S. Wright & Sons Ltd
Coles Farm Works
Boreham Road
Great Leighs
Chelmsford CM3 1PR
01245 361639

WOOD TURNER
Robin Wood
Lee Farm Cottage
Upper Booth
Edale
Derbyshire S30 2ZJ
01433 670321

YEOMAN RAVEN MASTER
David Cope
Tower of London
London EC3N 4AB
0171 488 5662

USEFUL ASSOCIATIONS AND ORGANIZATIONS

BASKETMAKERS'
ASSOCIATION
Pond Cottage
North Road
Amersham
Buckinghamshire HP6 5NA
01494 726189

BRITISH CARTOGRAPHIC
SOCIETY
c/o Mr Frank Blakeway
53 Rownhams Road
Maybush
Southampton SO16 5DX
01703 781519

BRITISH FIELD
SPORTS SOCIETY
367 Kennington Road
London SE11 4PT
0171 582 5432

BRITISH HAT GUILD
Business Centre
Kimpton Road
Luton
Bedfordshire LU2 0LB
01582 23456

BRITISH JEWELLERS'
ASSOCIATION
10 Vyse Street
Birmingham B18 6LT
0121 236 2657

BRITISH LEATHER
CONFEDERATION
Leather Trade House
King's Park Road
Moulton Park
Northampton NN3 6JD
01604 494131

BRITISH PRINTING
SOCIETY
BM/ISPA
London WC1N 3XX
01252 26771

BRITISH SUNDIAL
SOCIETY
112 Whitehall Road
Chingford
London E4 6DW
0181 529 4880

BRITISH TOY
MAKERS' GUILD
124 Walcott Street
Bath BA1 5BG
01225 442440

CONTEMPORARY
GLASS SOCIETY
7 The Leather Markets
Weston Street
London SE1 3ER
0171 403 2800

CORACLE SOCIETY
c/o Vivien Faulkner
24 Watling Street
Leintwardine
Shropshire SY7 0LW
01547 540629

COUNTRY LIFE
King's Reach Tower
Stamford Street
London SE1 9LS
0171 261 7058

CRAFTS COUNCIL
44a Pentonville Road
Islington
London N1 9BY
0171 278 7700

DRYSTONE WALLING
ASSOCIATION OF
GREAT BRITAIN
c/o YFC Centre
National Agricultural Centre
Stoneleigh Park
Kenilworth
Warwickshire CV8 2LG
Fax: 0121 378 0493

EMBROIDERERS' GUILD
Apartment 41
Hampton Court Palace
Surrey KT8 9AU
0181 943 1229

GUILD OF INTERNATIONAL
BUTLER ADMINISTRATORS
AND PERSONAL ASSISTANTS
12 Little Bornes
Dulwich
London SE21 8SE
0181 670 5585

KITE SOCIETY
PO Box 2274
Great Horkesley
Colchester
Essex CO6 4AY
01206 271489

LONDON MASTER
PLASTERERS' ASSOCIATION
18 Mansfield Street
London W1M 9FG
0171 580 5404

NATIONAL ASSOCIATION
OF FARRIERS AND
BLACKSMITHS
Avenue B
10th Street
NAC
Stoneleigh
Warwickshire CV8 2LG
01203 696595

NATIONAL COUNCIL FOR
THE CONSERVATION OF
PLANTS AND GARDENS
The Pines
RHS Garden
Wisley
Woking
Surrey GU23 6QP
01483 211465

NATIONAL
HEDGELAYING SOCIETY
c/o YFC Centre
National Agricultural Centre
Stoneleigh Park
Kenilworth
Warwickshire CV8 2LG
01203 696544

ROYAL HORTICULTURAL
SOCIETY
80 Vincent Square
London SW1P 2PE
0171 834 4333

SCOTTISH TARTAN
SOCIETY
Port-na-Craig
Pitlochry PH16 5ND
01796 474079

SOCIETY OF
BOTANICAL ARTISTS
1 Knapp Cottage
Wyke
Gillingham
Dorset SP8 4NQ
01747 825718

SOCIETY OF
HERALDIC ARTS
46 Reigate Road
Reigate
Surrey RH2 0QN
01737 242945

SOCIETY OF
MINIATURISTS
41 Lister Street
Riverside Gardens
Ilkley
West Yorkshire LS29 9ET
01943 609075

SOCIETY OF
PLOUGHMEN LTD
Quarry Farm
Loversall
Doncaster DN11 9DH
01302 852469

SPECIALIST
CHEESEMAKERS'
ASSOCIATION
PO Box 448
Newcastle-under-Lyme
Staffordshire ST5 0BF
01782 582597

UNITED KINGDOM
HARP ASSOCIATION
c/o D. Edling
PO Box 3069
London WC2H 8JD
0171 836 9181

If you require further information about Britain's Living National Treasures, please call Country Life's *Treasures hotline on 0171 261 7085 or write to* Country Life, *King's Reach Tower, Stamford Street, London SE1 9LS*

Index

A

Ackrill, Victor 130
Acton, Thomas 114
Albeck, Pat 112
Allen, Ken 122
Allen, Roy 122
Architectural Draughtsman 54
Artist in Glass 118

B

Baga, Ena 115
Bagpipe Maker 128
Bailey, Nelson 118
Bait Digger 131
Bampton, Russell 131
Bar Manager 123
Barber, Paul 124
Barometer Specialist 116
Barrett, Allan 110
Barrow, Rex 126
Basford, Andy and David 120
Basket Maker 118
Batchelor, John 125
Bates, Brian 131
Batman 127
Bell Founder 32
Bellows Maker 92
Bennett-Levy, Valerie 117
Bicknell, David and Robert 36
Blade Cutter 130
Boiler Maker 36
Bookbinder 66
Boorman, Philip 121
Boot-Tree Maker 90
Booth, Raymond 124
Botanical Artist 124
Boustead, Neil 123
Braimbridge, Elizabeth 16
Brears, Peter 127
Breeches Maker 115
Brennan, Ian 116
Brick Maker 26
Broch Maker 98
Bronze Founder 60
Broom Squire 94
Brown, Maureen 117
Brush Maker 129
Builder 130

Bunyan, Sybil 119
Burdett, Will 115
Butcher 116
Butcher, Anne Marie 130
Butler 50

C

Caley, Trevor 130
Canal Boatman 123
Ceremonial-Badge Maker 124
Chalmers, Louis 118
Chapman, Eddie 128
Chapman, Norman 113
Cheese Maker 113
Childs, Leonard 113
Clayton, Tony 121
Clifford, Kathleen 48
Clog Maker 118
Coach Painter 131
Coat Maker 46
Cobley, Tom 123
Coke, Peter 126
Congdon, Robin 113
Cooper 96
Cooper, Malcolm 117
Cope, David 120
Coppicer .119
Coracle Maker 102
Corne, Ray 44
Country-House Painter 56
Cox, Peter 127
Crellin, Michael 126
Cresser, Robert 129
Cricket-Bat Maker 114
Crutchley, Anna 126
Cuirass and Helmet Maker 120
Cutts, Mike 125

D

Damascus-Barrel Maker 124
Daniels, George 127
Donald, John 124
Doyle, Nancy 123
Drystone Waller 22
Duck Breeder 124
Durno, Bruce 40
Dutch, Arthur 130

E

Ecclesiastical Embroiderer 113
Edwards, Eric 104
Embroiderer 130
Enamel Artist 129

F

Farrier 38
Faulkener, Peter 102
Finedon, Gary 119
Fish Smoker 114
Fly-Tyer 121
Foggitt, Bill 18
Food Historian 127
Forbes, William 88
Fountain-Pen Repairer 84
Freeminer 24
Fruit-Tree Trainer 128
Furniture Maker 121

G

Games Maker 74
Gardener .114
Garnett, Keith 30
Garnham, Piers 121
Garnons Williams, John 125
Gatt, Hector 116
Gilder and Carver 58
Gin Noser 112
Glass Engraver 113
Glass-Thermometer Blower 130
Glasshouse Maker 120
Glue, Gregor 119
Golf-Club Maker 119
Gower, Victor 123
Grandison, Leonard 64
Gregory, Charlie 90
Groom, Duncan 131
Grotto Builder 115
Groundsman 115
Gun-Case Maker 114
Gun Maker 120
Gypsy-Caravan Restorer 118

H

Hall, George and Thomas 22
Hamilton, Duncan 125
Hand Stitcher 119

Handle Bender 124
Harness Maker 113
Harpist 108
Harrison, Nick 126
Hawk-Furniture Maker 112
Hay-Rake Maker 34
Hayward, John 126
Head, Henry 127
Head, John 123
Hedgelayer 117
Hepburn, Danny and Gordon 116
Heraldic Sculptor 116
Historical Cartographer 125
Hodges, Albert 50
Hogarth, Bill 119
Hook, George 100
Hooker Builder 116
Horticultural-Show Manager 114
House, Jack 20
House of Lords Doorkeeper 129
Hughes, Sir David 122
Hulme, Roger 72
Human, Ryan 116
Hunt Tailor 129
Huntsman 40

I

Ice Sculptor 125
Ingram, Peter 118
Irish, Joe .113

J

Jackson, George and Rosemary . . .114
Jacques, Christopher 74
Jewel Setter 120
Jones, Dennis 120
Jones, John 92

K

Keeling, Jim 70
Keely, Tim 114
Kendal Mint-Cake Maker 129
Kerr, Barry 119
Kite Maker 126
Knell, Ted 60

L

Ladies' Taylor 122
Lane, Stan 78
Larter, Gilbert 130
Lavender Farmer 127
Laver-Gibbs, Christine 122
Lawson, John 120
Leary, Craig 113
Leather Worker 127
Levett, Keith 46
Littler, Kenneth 114
Loe, Ian 121
Lord's Dinner Lady 123

M

McAtasney, John 122
McKay Brown, David 120
McNiff, Frank 128
McPhillips, Frankie 121
McWilliams, Sidney 128
Marbler 119
Marden, Pat 128
Margan, Paul 114
Marney, Patrick 116
Marshman 104
Mascot Maker 122
Master Bowyer 123
Matholus, Danny 32
Middleton, Ken 120
Miller 121
Miller, Eddie 124
Millstone Dresser 117
Milner, Frank and Roger 42
Miniaturist 117
Model Maker 52
Mole Catcher 125
Moore, Hamish 128
Mortimer, Ian 80
Mosaicist 130
Mount Cutter 131
Mulkerrins, Colm 116
Mulvany, Kevin 52
Munson, James 108
Myles-Lea, Jonathan 56

N

Nail Maker 28
Nash, Arthur 94
Nelson, Jeremy 118
Nicholls, Jeff 125
Nurseryman 127

O

Officer of Arms 124
Oliver, Neil 82
Ornamenter 131

P

Palmer, Christine 58
Paper Maker 122
Parchment Maker 68
Pargeter 62
Parkinson, Peter 114
Parry, Bob 127
Pearl Worker 100
Penknife Cutler 86
Pickford, Sue 129
Pierce, Michael 117
Plasterer 64
Ploughman 20
Plume Maker 118
Pocock, Betty and Peter 125
Polo-Stick Maker 119
Pondkeeper 128
Ponton, John 115
Poppy Maker 128
Posy Maker 117
Potter 70
Poultry Breeder 115
Printer 80
Pritchard, Alan 123
Prosser, Lilian 128
Pub-Sign Painter 122
Purse, Raymond 117
Puzzle Maker 76

R

Raffle, Andrew and David 14
Rare-Plant Conservator 16
Rea, Rupert 23
Read, George 122
Read, Terence 127
Reeves, Mike 98
Revell, Keith 122
Reynell, Diana 115
Reyntiens, Patrick 118
Ribbon Worker 117
Riding-Hat Maker 44
Rigger 30
Ripley, Peter 129
Roads, Elizabeth 124
Rocking-Horse Maker 123
Rogers, Russell 118

Rogers, Susan 52
Rolls-Royce Builder 120
Rope Maker 113
Rowlatt, Christopher 119
Rudd, John 34
Rugby-Ball Maker 125
Rustic-Hut Maker 14

S

Saddler 42
Sausage Maker 116
Sawyer 118
Scott, Ted 130
Seal Maker 82
Seat Weaver 126
Secateur Repairer 121
Shaw, Stan 86
Sheet-Metal Worker 130
Shell Artist 126
Silent-Film Pianist 115
Silversmith 125
Simms, Alastair 96
Skelton, Richard 129
Slate River 126
Smith, Michael 115
Snigger 122
Spicer, Sarah 131
Split-Cane Rod Maker 106
Stamp Artist 121
Stanton Laurence 106
Stationery Engraver 115
Stilton Maker 129
Stocker, Peter 76
Sundial Maker 114
Sweetingham, Mavis 114

T

Tanner 117
Tartan Weaver 119
Tassel Maker 126
Taxidermist 88
Tea Importer 128
Tea-Towel Designer 112
Terrier Breeder 128
Thatcher 12
Thornton, Eric 128
Throssell, Eric 54
Tidmarsh, Bernard 38
Timmins, Daniel 46
Timms, George and John 115
Toffee Maker 123

Top-Hat Maker 72
Topping, Bill 66
Tram Superintendent 126
Tunks, Peter 117
Turbitt, David and Frank 12
Typographer 78

U

Umbrella Maker 113
Upton, Roger 112

V

Village Shopkeeper 125
Vintage-Car Builder 121
Visscher, Wim 68

W

Waller, Richard 124
Wallpaper Maker 110
Watch Maker 127
Watkinson, Bill 26
Weatherman 18
Weaver 122
Welsh, Stephen 62
Whisky Brewer 116
Whistler, Laurence 113
Wig Maker 48
Willder, Sam 129
Williams, Hugh 112
Willow Merchant 131
Wiper, Harry 129
Wood, Robin 131
Wood Turner 131
Wright, Carlton 131
Wright, Jonathan and Ray 24

Y

Yeoman Raven Master 120

Z

Zeegan, Irene 113
Zeff, Roy 84

Acknowledgements

Grateful thanks to
Camilla Bonn, Camilla Costello,
Paula Fahey, Michael Lyons, Ann O'Neill, Tracey Tucker,
Rupert Uloth, Isambard Wilkinson.
Special thanks to Rachel Pearce at
the IPC Book Department.

Picture Credits

The photographs in this book are by Simon Upton, with the exception of:

Bell Founder, page 33 Julian Nieman;

Boiler Maker, page 37 Craig Knowles;

Coracle Maker, page 103 Alex Ramsay;

Hooker Builder, page 116 Mark Fiennes;

Yeoman Raven Master, page 120 Julian Nieman;

Fly-Tyer, page 121 Mike England;

Ladies' Tailor, page 122 Julian Nieman;

Weaver, page 122 Mike England;

Tram Superintendent, page 126 Mike England;

Slate River, page 126 Mike England;

Watchmaker, page 127 Mike England;

Batman, page 127 William Shaw;

Lavender Farmer, page 127 June Buck;

Fruit-Tree Trainer, page 128 David Giles;

Pond Keeper, page 128 Craig Knowles;

Tea Importer, page 128 Mike England;

Bagpipe Maker, page 98 Simon Jauncey;

Poppy Maker, page 128 David Banks;

Brush Maker, page 129 Simon Jauncey;

Kendal Mint-Cake Maker, page 129 Mike England;

Hunt Tailor, page 129 David Giles;

Stilton Maker, page 129 Craig Knowles;

Enamel Artist, page 129 David Banks;

Mosaicist, page 130, David Giles;

Embroiderer, page 130 David Banks;

Blade Cutter, page 130 Craig Knowles;

Builder, page 130 Clive Boursnell;

Glass-Thermometer Blower, page 130 Craig Knowles;

Metal Worker, page 130 Simon Jauncey;

Wood Turner, page 131 David Giles;

Willow Merchant, page 131 Craig Knowles;

Ornamenter, page 131 David Giles;

Bait Digger, page 131 Guy Mansell;

Coach Painter, page 131 Clive Boursnell.

9 1999